ESSENTIAL  MANAGERS

BALANCING WORK AND LIFE

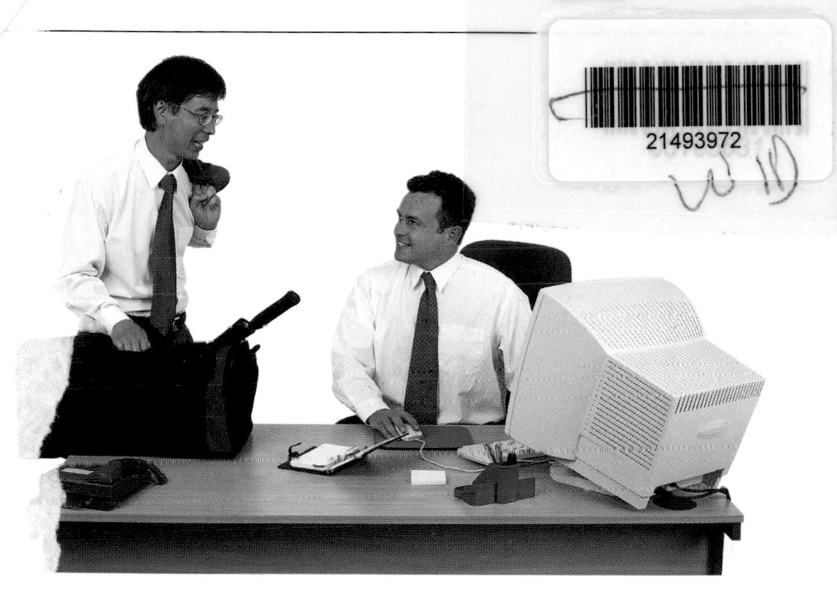

ROBERT HOLDEN
& BEN RENSHAW

LONDON, NEW YORK, MUNICH,
MELBOURNE, DELHI

Senior Editors Amy Corzine
and Jacky Jackson
Senior Art Editor Sarah Cowley
DTP Designers Julian Dams
Production Manager Michelle Thomas

Managing Editor Adèle Hayward
Managing Art Editor Karen Self

Produced for Dorling Kindersley by

studio **cactus**

13 SOUTHGATE STREET WINCHESTER HAMPSHIRE SO23 9DZ

Editor Kate Hayward
Designer Laura Watson

First published in Great Britain in 2002 by
Dorling Kindersley Limited,
80 Strand
London, WC2R ORL

A Penguin Company

2 4 6 8 10 9 7 5 3 1

A CIP catalogue record for this book is available from the British Library

ISBN 0 7513 35711

Reproduced by Colourscan, Singapore
Printed and bound in Hong Kong by Wing King Tong

See our complete catalogue at
www.dk.com

CONTENTS

Understanding Yourself

Making Changes

Sustaining Balance

INTRODUCTION

All too often, success is seen in terms of material possessions and financial gain. It is easy to fall into the trap of working long hours, striving to achieve a good standard of living but, in the process, neglecting relationships, self-development, leisure pursuits, and personal happiness. Balancing Work and Life *will help you understand what success means to you and explains how you can live your life with renewed vision and purpose. Practical advice, including 101 concise tips, shows you how to focus on your true priorities and develop healthy attitudes to success in yourself and your team. As you begin to achieve a better balance in your work and life, you will discover new levels of creativity, fulfilment, and happiness.*

ASSESSING SUCCESS

To be successful in your work and life, you must be clear about what success is. Clarify your values and goals, and understand that success is not just about hard work and no play.

UNDERSTANDING SUCCESS

To create a balance between the demands of your work and your life, you need to examine what success means to you. Start by clarifying your values, purpose, roles, and attitudes so that you have something to measure your achievements against.

Think about what success means to you – be honest with yourself.

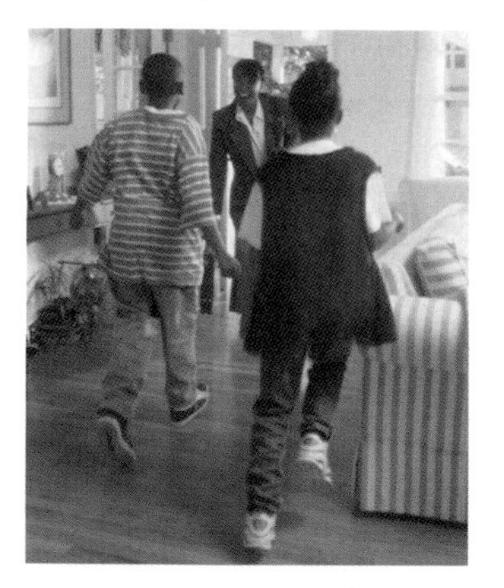

DEFINING SUCCESS

People often work hard to gain "success" without knowing what success really means. You may climb a career ladder, but are you fulfilled by your work? Do you have a good home life? We receive differing messages about success – through the media, our families, and our culture. But ultimately, success comes from leading a fulfilled and balanced life. Begin to balance your work and life more effectively.

◀ **RECOGNIZING SUCCESS**
A successful person has a clear definition of success. This manager enjoys her job, but she leaves the office on time so that she can spend time with her family.

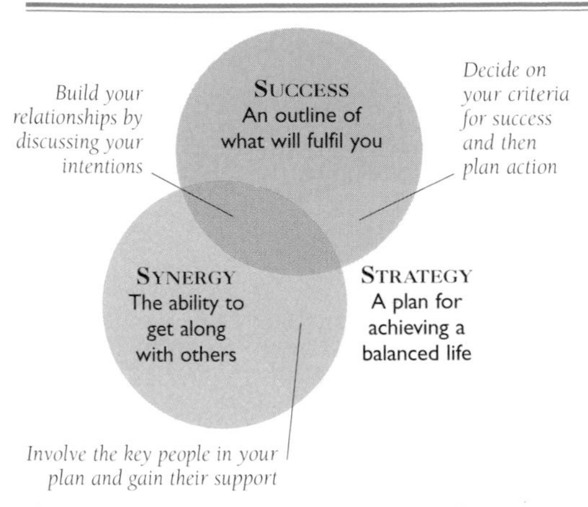

▲ ACHIEVING A BALANCED LIFE
Develop criteria for success so that you can focus on your priorities. Form a strategy to help you stay on track, and focus on synergy so that you have the necessary support to achieve success.

AIMING FOR SUCCESS

The "S^3" formula will help you consider the key factors in a work-life balance. The first "S" stands for "Success" – begin to form criteria of what success means to you. The second "S" stands for "Strategy" – start to form a workable plan to achieve a balance between work and life. The third "S" denotes "Synergy" – make sure you focus on relationships and creative co-operation with those around you. Aim to be a team player and a good communicator.

CLARIFYING VALUES

To define success, start by clarifying your values. Schedule time alone and think about what is most important to you. What kind of partner and parent do you want to be? What kind of son or daughter? What kind of friend and manager? What difference would you like to make in people's lives? Put your values at the centre of your life so that you can retain greater balance, vision, and happiness in every area of your life.

FOCUSING ON VALUES ▶
Think about the relationships you have with others and what you most value about them. Decide on the characteristics that you value in yourself.

2 Set time aside every day to focus on your values, and ensure that you remain true to them.

CHOOSING A PURPOSE

Purpose is your reason for doing something: it is what gives your work and life meaning. Purpose is something that you choose rather than find, and it is based on what is important to you. For example, if being a loving parent and a supportive colleague is what is important to you, then your purpose may be to inspire others with your strength of character. If it is important to you to achieve certain work goals, then your purpose may be to be an effective role model to your team. Pinpoint your purpose so that you have real direction.

QUESTIONS TO ASK YOURSELF

Q What aspects of my life am I most passionate about?

Q Is being a parent the most important aspect of my life?

Q Have I recognized what motivates me?

Q What are my unique talents and my strengths?

Q What purpose would I like to give my work and my life?

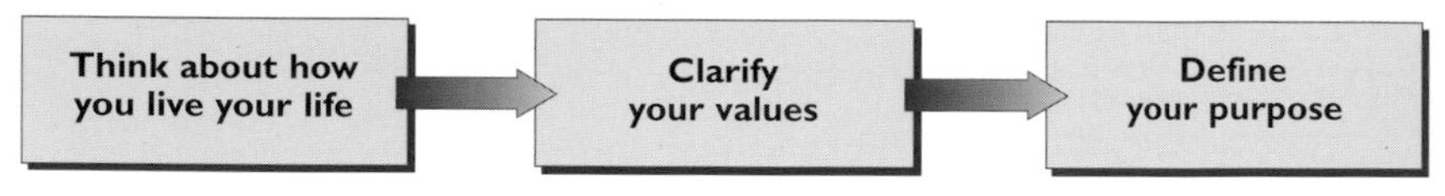

▲ BECOMING FOCUSED
Think deeply about each aspect of your life and work. This will help you reach a better understanding of your values, and enable you to focus on your purpose.

3 Make the time to create a picture of your ideal life.

SEEING THE BIG PICTURE

The big picture is your overall vision of your work and life. It includes your values, goals, and roles. Invest time in developing your vision. Allow your imagination free rein and picture your ideal life. Picture the key people in your life – your family, friends, colleagues, and customers – and imagine all these relationships working well. Visualize your ideal work and your ideal leisure time. Write down the essence of your big picture.

Puts together a picture of key factors in his life

BUILDING A PICTURE ▶
Cut out photographs and images to make a blueprint of your ideal life and collate them together on a board.

RECOGNIZING SUCCESS AS A STATE OF MIND

Success is an attitude, and not just a set of achievements or financial gain. If this were not the case, then every high achiever would consider themselves successful. But, in fact, many rich, famous, and accomplished people have material success but do not actually feel truly successful or fulfilled. Understand that success is not just found in outer things, but is located within yourself. Cultivate success as a state of mind so that you stop chasing false goals and expectations, and start living your life focused on what matters to you.

Develop a positive attitude towards achieving success.

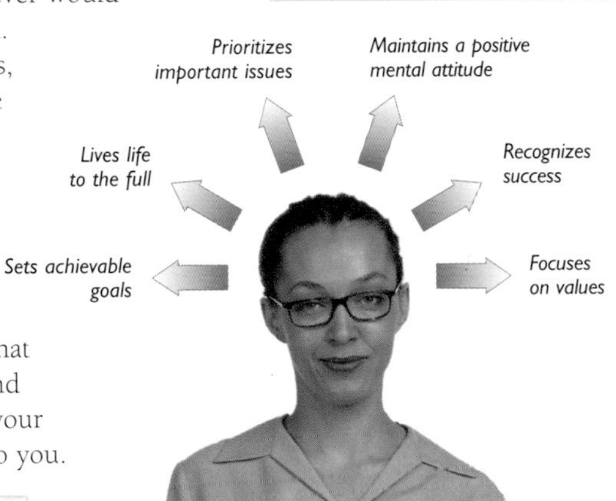

5 **Involve your family in the development of your vision.**

▲ **HAVING THE RIGHT ATTITUDE**

It is important to have a positive, proactive attitude so that you can live your life with purpose and vision. This will enable you to increase your effectiveness and achieve success and fulfilment.

CASE STUDY

The managing director of a clothing outlet had achieved the trappings of success. He had a lifestyle that friends admired: a substantial income, a large house, a fast car, and he enjoyed annual luxury holidays.

Unfortunately, he neither felt successful, nor enjoyed his achievements – his marriage was collapsing, his children no longer confided in him, and he was constantly under pressure to expand his business.

When he actually evaluated his definition of success, he discovered that he valued his family, friends, and leisure time more than his business.

He developed a strategy that incorporated his true priorities. He explained to his colleagues that he would be leaving work on time to see his family and pursue other interests. As he began to resolve his family conflicts and rekindle a zest for life, he found that he began to enjoy his work more too.

◀ **EVALUATING SUCCESS**

In this case study, a managing director saw that his family life was being damaged by his constant striving for financial success. By involving his family and friends in developing a new vision, he was able to live his life with renewed purpose.

AT WHAT COST SUCCESS?

In a fast, busy world, you pay a high price for confusing success with constant adrenaline, endless activity, all work, no rest, and no play. Avoid working long hours to meet deadlines, learn how to manage your time, and avoid falling into an activity trap.

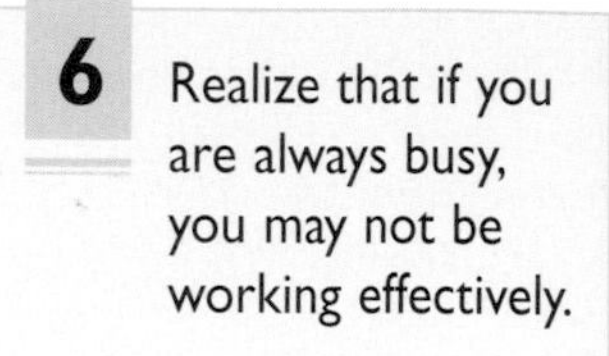

QUESTIONS TO ASK YOURSELF

- **Q** Do I work longer hours than I need to?
- **Q** Am I achieving something important or am I just keeping busy?
- **Q** Do I feel guilty if I am the first person to leave the office?
- **Q** How can I prioritize my time more effectively?

MANAGING YOUR TIME

One of the biggest traps to fall into today is the "busy culture". The major problem with this culture is that the habit of "busy-ness" eclipses real business: it gives rise to a "start early, finish late" work ethic that confuses constant effort with real effectiveness. Avoid keeping busy out of a sense of habit, duty, or guilt – these factors all reduce effectiveness, morale, and motivation. Think about how you could be less busy and more effective. How could you work smarter, not harder?

MANAGING URGENCY

If you are always busy, you may not have the time to prioritize effectively. You may waste time on urgent tasks rather than concentrating on what is important. An urgent task is something that requires immediate attention. Importance, on the other hand, has to do with the big picture, core values, and your purpose. Have the courage to put priorities first, even when you are under pressure, so that you build success in the long-term.

7 Prioritize tasks according to their importance, not their urgency, so that you always stay focused.

PRIORITIZING TIME

Recognize that you are overloaded with urgent tasks

↓

Look at the tasks that are critical and must be done

↓

Decide which tasks can be put on hold or delegated

↓

Concentrate on the critical tasks and work more effectively

LIVING TOO FAST

Many results today are measured in terms of speed. However, although speed is important for factors such as strategy or service, it must not override everything. Speed of delivery, for example, must be balanced with quality of work, and an upgrade to faster technology must be led by vision and not just for the sake of change itself. Although you may enjoy living life in the fast lane, realize that there are costs in terms of your health and wellbeing. Remember that relationships can deteriorate if they are not given time and attention.

8 Remember that speed can detract from quality.

9 Be alert to the symptoms of burnout.

RECOGNIZING BURNOUT

People suffering from burnout often have identifiable characteristics, such as chronic fatigue, a short fuse, impaired vision, poor productivity, and low self-esteem. Sufferers may withdraw from family and friends, or seek escape through alcoholism, absenteeism, or illness.

THE ACTIVITY TRAP

Constant activity is a trap that erodes effectiveness at work and in life. Temper your drive to be active with moments of reflection so that you can achieve a sense of accomplishment. All too often, in an effort to achieve a result, we damage a relationship, neglect what's important, and cause unnecessary distress. Always clarify your priorities before taking action.

AVOIDING WORKAHOLISM

Workaholism is an escape from life through work. It is a compulsive behaviour that can damage effectiveness, estrange families, and impair health. A workaholic will ensure that they always have access to work. Often confused as a sign of dedication, this leads to imbalance and burnout. Be alert to symptoms of overload and focus on balancing your work and life.

▼ REACHING OVERLOAD
This manager is struggling to deal with a number of tasks at once and is unable to focus and prioritize.

Receives message from customer on his mobile phone

Cancels social plans at last minute

CREATING CRITERIA

A healthy work–life balance is achieved by establishing clear criteria for success that include work objectives, leisure plans, and aims for self-improvement. Take an honest look at your priorities and set goals that you can work towards.

10 Make sure that your work is led by your criteria for success.

11 Take your interests outside work seriously.

12 Ask your friends and family what success means to them.

SUCCEEDING AT WORK

Think deeply about your criteria for success at work. Is your criteria to get the job done at whatever cost? Does the means justify the end? What sort of work relationships do you want? Reflect upon the impact work has on the rest of your life. Does work enrich the whole of your life or has your home life become merely a rest from work? Each day, ask yourself, "How do I know if I have been successful at work or not?" Be specific. Think about the quality of your relationships. How important is your self-development and learning? Start to write down your criteria.

CASE STUDY

A manager in the hospitality industry was having difficulty coping with his work.

He decided to pinpoint his priorities and write down his goals for his work and life. He found that this enabled him to manage his workload. Even if he was faced with a difficult task, he discovered that he was able to cope because he had a clear criteria for success.

He decided that if he needed to attend his children's school, he would make sure that he was available. At the same time, he worked at maintaining good friendships. Meanwhile, his self-regulation meant that he spent more time on the important aspects of his work, such as meeting customers' needs and encouraging team morale.

Since he was now performing to his new high standards, he become a sought-after hospitality manager whilst enjoying a balanced home life.

◀ **REMAINING FOCUSED**
This manager found that strong commitment to his roles and goals, and an ability to remain focused, were deciding factors in his success.

IDENTIFYING ROLES

A role defines an area of responsibility, such as being a manager, parent, partner, or friend. To enjoy a healthy work–life balance you must define each of your roles. Be careful not to neglect your most important roles. For example, be aware that your role as a parent can be damaged if you consistently prioritize your work above your family. Your role as a husband or a wife can suffer if you spend too much time and energy on your career or your children. And friendships can be lost if you do not make the time to pick up the phone. Be clear and flexible in your roles.

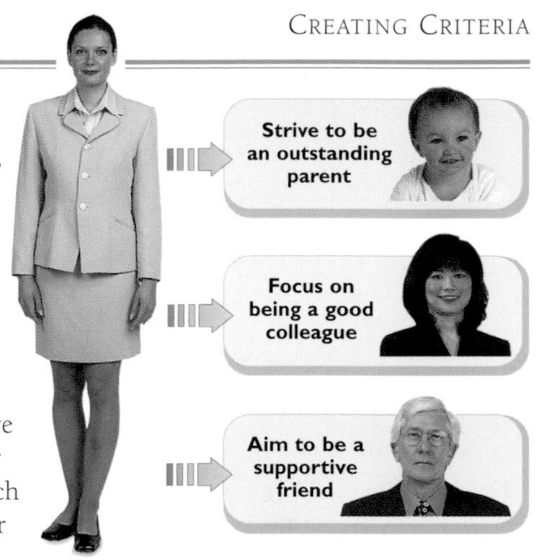

▲ DEFINING YOUR ROLES

Think about the critical roles in your life. When you are setting your criteria for success, consider what you want to achieve in these roles so that you can excel in them.

13 List, prioritize, and assess the important roles you play in your work and in your life.

SUCCEEDING IN LIFE

Think about your life as a whole – your family, friends, leisure pursuits, personal development goals, and involvement in your community. How significant a part do you want to play in the development of your children? What do you consider to be success in your friendships? What are your favourite leisure pursuits? What are your personal development goals? Realize that success is about all aspects of life, and not just about work.

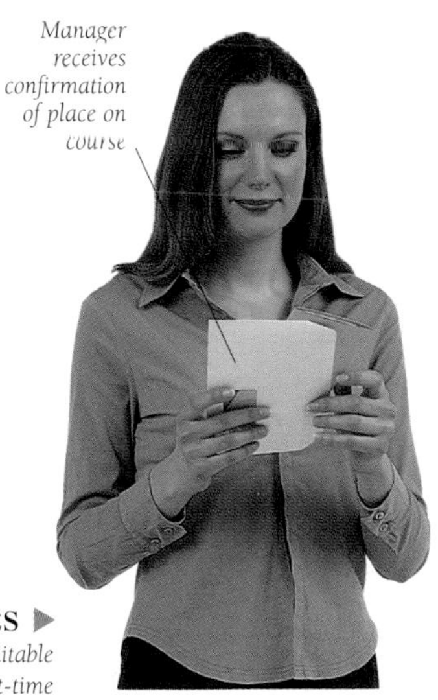

CONTINUING YOUR STUDIES ▶

If your priority is to further your education, look for a suitable course at a college. This manager wants to continue part-time academic studies while she continues working.

SETTING GOALS

Setting your short-, mid-, and long-term goals is essential when it comes to creating clear criteria for success. Write down your goals in three main categories: things you want to be, things you hope to do, and things you wish to have. Use the SMART formula to help you work through the process. Be Specific: state your goals precisely and clearly. Make sure they are Measurable – ensure that you can obtain proof of your progress and can check that you are on track. Set achievable Actions – state what tasks need to be carried out. Be Realistic – make sure your goals are a possible dream. Allow for Timing – allocate a reasonable time span for each goal.

SMART GOALS

SPECIFIC
Ensure your aim is clear

MEASURABLE
Define standards to work to

ACTIONS
Set yourself tasks to do

REALISTIC
Make sure the goal is achievable

TIMING
Set a time frame

LISTING A SET OF GOALS

A successful manager has clearly defined her goals on paper. The act of writing these goals down focused her mind and reflected her commitment to achieving them.

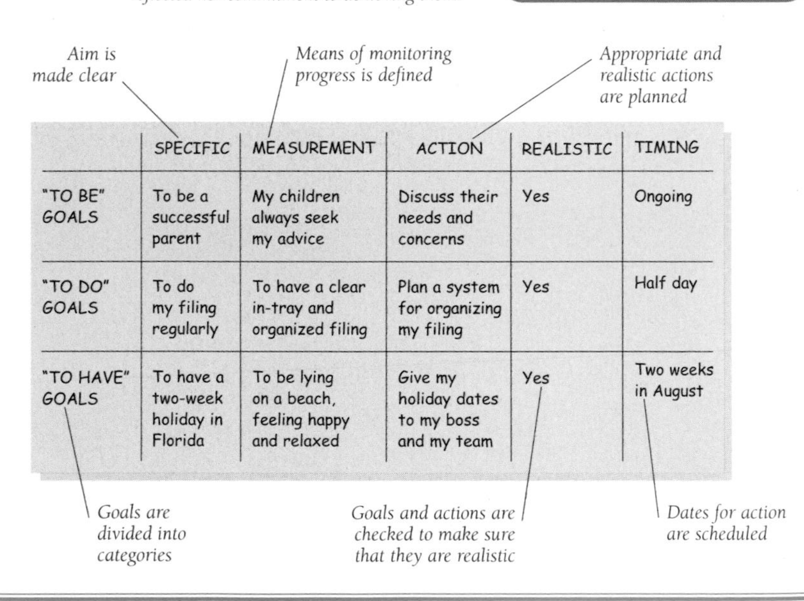

	SPECIFIC	MEASUREMENT	ACTION	REALISTIC	TIMING
"TO BE" GOALS	To be a successful parent	My children always seek my advice	Discuss their needs and concerns	Yes	Ongoing
"TO DO" GOALS	To do my filing regularly	To have a clear in-tray and organized filing	Plan a system for organizing my filing	Yes	Half day
"TO HAVE" GOALS	To have a two-week holiday in Florida	To be lying on a beach, feeling happy and relaxed	Give my holiday dates to my boss and my team	Yes	Two weeks in August

14 Think about tasks you are good at and aim to build on your strengths.

PRIORITIZING KEY ISSUES

Make sure that you prioritize your goals, your strengths, and your actions. Recognize that you cannot excel at everything and prioritize accordingly. If necessary, delegate those tasks or issues that do not complement your skills. Ask yourself, "What am I really good at?", "Where do my natural talents lie?", "What do I enjoy most?", and "What will help me advance my life's goals and vision?" Being strategic about key issues at work and in your life will make all the difference to achieving a healthy balance.

MAKING A SUCCESS STATEMENT

A success statement provides a reference point for assessing your work and life balance. Form one that encompasses your values and purpose. Include your roles and goals. The statement will become your personal constitution, the criterion by which you measure the balance of work and life. Involve a trusted friend or colleague in the process so that they can give you feedback. Let the statement inspire your decisions, influence your actions, and guide your life.

15 Write your success statement and refer to it regularly.

▼ WRITING A STATEMENT

In this example, a manager has written out a success statement. The statement is a live document that the manager can update and adapt regularly to ensure that it is still relevant.

MY SUCCESS STATEMENT

I choose a harmonious balance between my work and my life. I address my family's needs first, and I aim to contribute to their wellbeing, happiness, and sense of fulfilment. I am proactive in my work, and I achieve my career goals with imagination and integrity. I am known for my sense of humour and my compassion. I am a team player. I always celebrate the successes of my colleagues and partners. I am committed to learning something new every day. I enjoy quality leisure time, and I eat and sleep well. I am able to relax, and I celebrate life every day.

EVALUATING YOUR SUCCESS

Having established your criteria for success, the next step is to be able to measure it. Recognize the signs that show you that you are achieving success, ask your friends for feedback, and, if possible, work with a coach to keep your objectives clear.

16 Review your successes – make sure that you are ready to adapt.

THINGS TO DO

1. Put a date in your diary each week to review your successes.
2. Spend 30 minutes reviewing your achievements.
3. Make sure that you are meeting your criteria.

REVIEWING SUCCESS

Success is a process, not just a final goal. If you are going to achieve a balance between your work and life, you will need to monitor and review your progress constantly. Continually reflect on the big picture of your life so that you can make sure that your actions are relevant and you are using your time well. Schedule half an hour per week to review the factors that are critical to your success. Ensure that you stay committed to what is important to you.

MEASURING SUCCESS

What proof do you need to show you that you are succeeding in your work and your life? Would it involve receiving customer recognition? Does it include finishing projects and work on schedule? Would it be having a sense of purpose and fun at work? Or does it mean having time for your family and friends? Would it mean being able to play a game of golf a week? Would it involve having time for meditation? Make sure you know how you will measure success so that you remain motivated.

Director congratulates manager on successful results

RECOGNIZING SIGNS OF SUCCESS ▶
Think about how you will recognize signs of your success – this may be receiving praise from your boss if you have achieved good results on a project.

17 Ask for and learn from constructive feedback.

18 Use coaching to build strengths and overcome barriers.

RECEIVING FEEDBACK

A useful aid in measuring success is to receive feedback from colleagues, family, and friends. We all have skills we can improve, and these can often be more easily identified by others. Ask a trusted colleague to give you feedback on how to improve your effectiveness at work. Ask your partner or a trusted friend if they would give you feedback on your work–life balance. Be open-minded. Sometimes the truth is hard to hear, and sometimes new ideas are hard to adopt, but remember that positive feedback is a valuable gift.

WORKING WITH A COACH

Coaching is becoming increasingly popular because organizations are recognizing that long-term success depends on their staff – their level of commitment, expertise, and creativity. Working with a coach will enable you to clarify your work and life objectives. Realize that coaching can help you deal with difficult situations, such as work changes and personal problems. Use it to help you liberate your personal potential.

BEING COACHED ▶
Use a coaching session as an opportunity to assess your strengths and recognize your weaknesses so that you can build a successful future.

19 Think of one way you could improve your life every day and then take action.

DOS AND DON'TS

- ✔ Do make sure you reward yourself for your successes.
- ✔ Do ask your friends, partner, and colleagues for feedback on your work–life balance.
- ✘ Don't focus on your mistakes and ignore your successes.
- ✘ Don't underestimate the value of coaching in helping you to clarify your objectives.

ANALYZING YOUR SUCCESS

Find out how successful you are by responding to the following statements, and mark the options that are closest to your experience. Be as honest as you can: if your answer is "never", mark Option 1; if it is "always", mark Option 4, and so on. Add your scores together, and refer to the Analysis to see how you scored. Use your answers to identify areas that need most improvement.

OPTIONS

1 Never
2 Occasionally
3 Frequently
4 Always

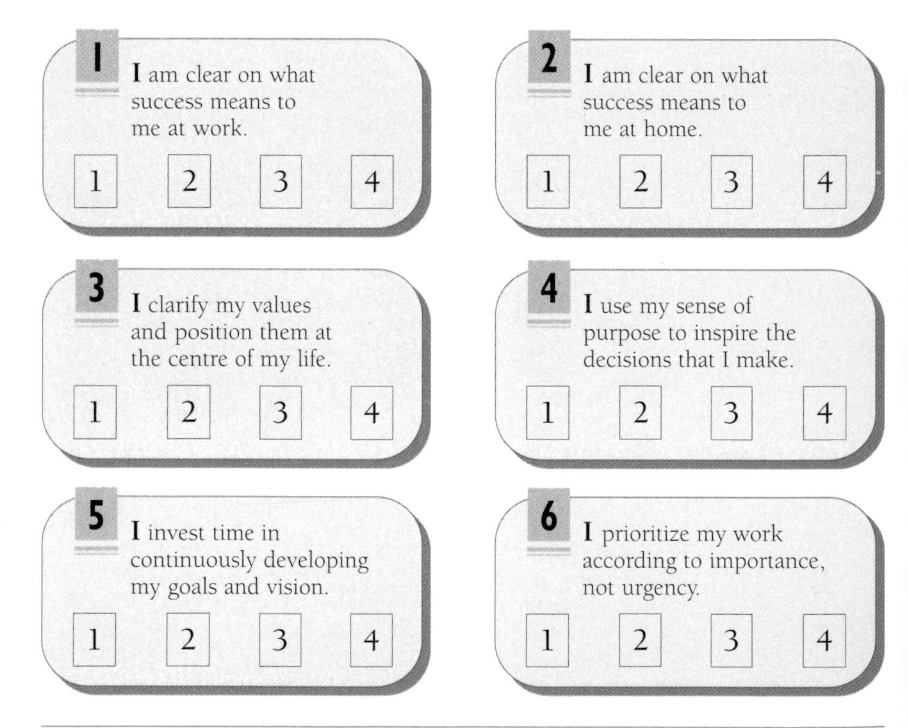

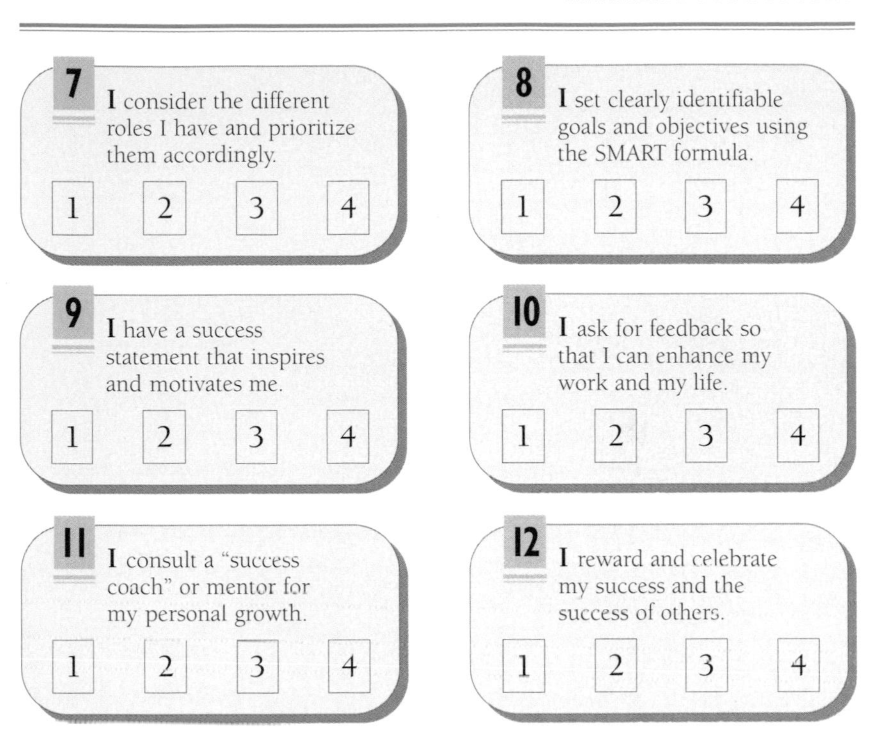

7 I consider the different roles I have and prioritize them accordingly.

1 2 3 4

8 I set clearly identifiable goals and objectives using the SMART formula.

1 2 3 4

9 I have a success statement that inspires and motivates me.

1 2 3 4

10 I ask for feedback so that I can enhance my work and my life.

1 2 3 4

11 I consult a "success coach" or mentor for my personal growth.

1 2 3 4

12 I reward and celebrate my success and the success of others.

1 2 3 4

Analysis

Now you have completed the self-assessment, add up your total score and check your performance by referring to the corresponding evaluation below. Identify your weakest areas, and refer to the relevant sections in this book where you will find practical advice and tips to help you focus on success:

12–23: You are surviving, but now it is time to thrive. You need to implement the strategies in this section to try something new and improve the balance of your work and life.

24–35: You are doing very well, but there is room for improvement and you can still achieve a better balance.

36–48: You are focused, well-motivated, good at motivating others, and have a clear sense of direction, both at home and at work. Keep this up.

UNDERSTANDING YOURSELF

Understanding yourself and what you want to achieve enables you to live a fulfilling life. Look at your beliefs, be sensitive to your emotions, assess your priorities, and plan action.

ANALYZING YOURSELF

Achieving a work–life balance involves challenging the way you think and behave. Use your beliefs, perceptions, choices, and actions in strategic ways to reach the balance you need. Think positively and take responsibility for your choices and decisions.

20 Make sure that you live your life by the values you believe in.

21 Develop beliefs that enhance your work–life balance.

UNDERSTANDING BELIEFS

You have beliefs about everything, including work, life, success, and happiness. These beliefs influence your choices and actions. It is often the case that people who have a poor work–life balance have limiting beliefs such as "success must have a price", "long hours are unavoidable", and "a social life comes later". Write down any limiting beliefs you hold and be as honest as possible.

WIDENING YOUR VISION ▼
Think about any assumptions you hold that may limit you, identify new options, and develop a new vision.

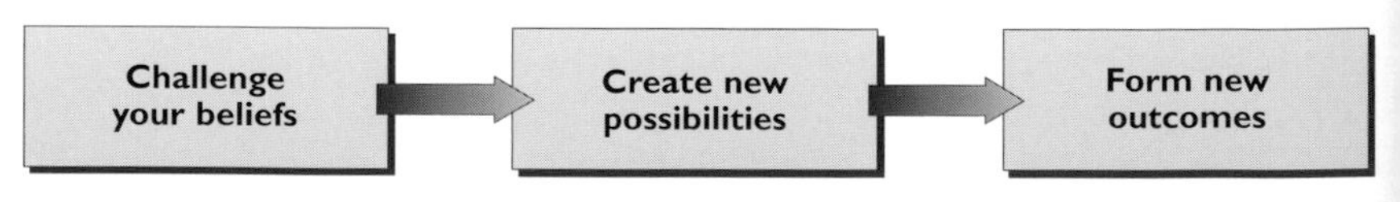

PERCEIVING CLEARLY

Perception is subjective and describes the way that you see things and the way you interpret experiences. Be aware that perception is a choice: there is always another way of seeing things. Change your perceptions and turn problems into opportunities, challenges into stepping stones, and setbacks into "set-ups" for greater success and happiness. Be prepared to look for solutions so that you will stand a good chance of finding them. Stay open and be flexible.

22 Think of new possibilities every day.

23 Start looking for better ways of doing things.

THINGS TO DO

1. Write down your thoughts about balancing work and life.
2. Identify the thoughts that limit your options.
3. Write down any new thoughts that you have about your life and review them regularly.

THINKING POSITIVELY

As the old saying states, "As a man thinketh, so he is". Psychologists estimate that people think approximately 40,000 thoughts per day and are responsible for choosing their thoughts. Try to put your past experiences and conditioning to one side so that you can create fresh ideas and lateral solutions – this is known as "possibility thinking". Be willing to let your old ideas make way for the new, because changing your thinking can change your life. Make sure that you help your team think positively rather than negatively too, because it will change the results they achieve.

COMPARING THINKING STYLES

THINKING NEGATIVELY	THINKING POSITIVELY
There is so much to do and there is never enough time to do it.	There is always enough time for what is really important.
People place too many demands on me. I cannot control my time.	I value my time and I can influence others to respect my needs.
I am busy, but I am not making a worthwhile contribution.	By being clear about success, I can make a real difference.

WATCHING YOUR WORDS

The most important conversations you hold in life are the ones that you hold with yourself. Notice how your "self-talk" influences your beliefs, choices, and actions. Start to listen to what you are telling yourself: listen for limiting "I can't" statements, "yes, but" affirmations, and "if only" self-talk. Make sure that you do not talk yourself out of what might be possible. Tell yourself that an effective work and life balance is a definite possibility and develop an "I can" mind-set. Adopt a new vocabulary that can help you overcome doubt, anxiety, cynicism, and tiredness.

24 Practise talking to yourself using positive language.

25 Learn to see the value of the contribution you make at work.

POINTS TO REMEMBER

- Changing your self-talk can change your life.
- The results you achieve depend on the choices and decisions that you make.
- You are responsible for the choices that you make, and you can take control of your work and life balance.

26 Think about the choices you make at work that affect your life.

MAKING CHOICES

People constantly make choices that influence their lives. It is easy to feel that you are not in control of your actions or your decisions, but the reality is that you are. For example, when your boss asks you to do something, make sure that you are in a position to carry out the request and be honest if you feel it is not feasible. Always consider the consequences of your choices for yourself and others – remember that your actions do not just affect you, they affect those around you.

Manager prepares to leave office

Boss stops him and asks him to attend meeting

TAKING CONTROL ▶

In this example, a manager is preparing to leave the office on time so that he can take his wife out for her birthday. When his boss asks him to attend a last-minute meeting, he has to act decisively.

TAKING ACTION

Taking action is about taking responsibility for your life. Do not blame circumstances, conditions, or others for your experiences. It is your choice either to wait for your life to get better, or to take action. The extent to which you are willing to act is equal to how far you are exercising your "proactivity muscle". Developing this "muscle" is comparable to working out at the gym – you cannot expect to develop strong biceps overnight. Practise creating a proactive mind-set and look for ways to enhance your life each day – then act!

Manager leaves office on time, happy with outcome

Boss understands and reschedules meeting

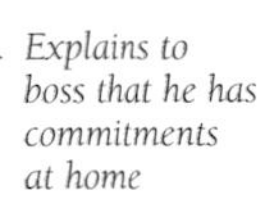

Explains to boss that he has commitments at home

Manager feels resentful – meeting is unproductive

UNDERSTANDING EMOTIONAL ISSUES

By improving your emotional intelligence, you can enjoy greater happiness and success in your relationships, your life, and your work. Recognize and learn from your emotions, be empathetic to others, and be ready to ask for support if necessary.

27 Recognize and understand your feelings so that you can act on them.

QUESTIONS TO ASK YOURSELF

- **Q** Do I listen to my feelings before I make a decision?
- **Q** Am I able to manage my feelings?
- **Q** Do I take into account the feelings of others?
- **Q** Are my actions always in tune with my values?
- **Q** Am I prepared to ask for the necessary support if I need guidance?

UNDERSTANDING EMOTIONAL INTELLIGENCE

Emotional intelligence is your ability to manage your feelings and thoughts. Developing your emotional intelligence can enhance your decision-making and help you communicate more honestly, think more clearly, and act more authentically. Be aware that your feelings are a gateway to creativity, intuition, and inspiration. If you can manage your feelings, you will manage yourself and others better. Realize that emotional intelligence helps you to tap into your own wisdom and develop understanding and trust in your relationships.

28 Take the time to listen to your feelings.

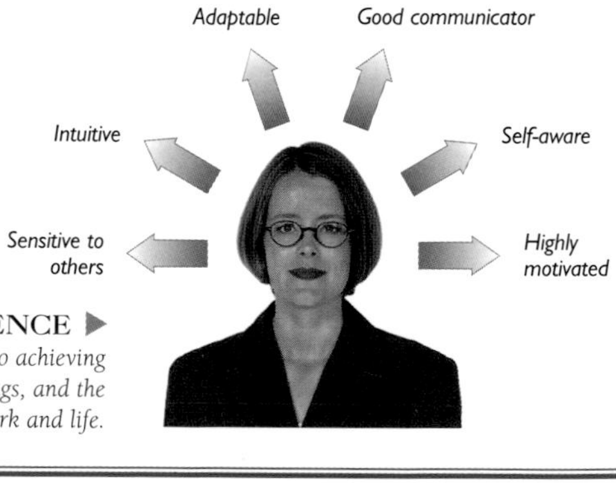

Adaptable
Good communicator
Intuitive
Self-aware
Sensitive to others
Highly motivated

EMOTIONAL INTELLIGENCE ▶
Being emotionally intelligent is the key to achieving success. By being aware of your own feelings, and the feelings of others, you can succeed in work and life.

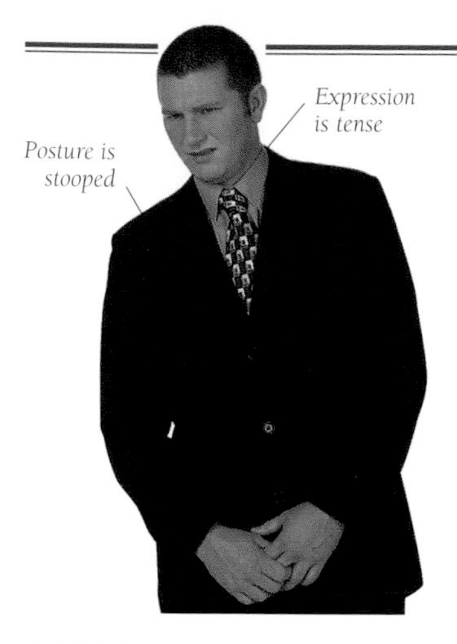

▲ **NOTICING EMOTIONS**
Learn to recognize the mental and physical signs of your emotions, and then you can act on them.

RECOGNIZING EMOTIONS

Take the time to record your thoughts and feelings every day – they can give you important insights. For example, monitoring your thoughts and feelings can help you see how well you are balancing your work and life. Notice when you feel confident and optimistic – this is a sign that you are doing well. Feelings of uncertainty and irritability may show that you are having difficulties. Realize that suppressing an emotion only blocks your learning and inhibits your self-awareness. Try to see something positive in all your emotions.

29 Be constructive and learn from your feelings, rather than ignoring them or indulging in them.

LEARNING FROM EMOTIONS

Emotions are pieces of information. They are messages that you can read and learn from to help you achieve greater success and happiness. For example, stress might be an invitation to change something; pain might be a signal to let go of something; fear might be a sign that you need extra help; doubt might be encouraging you to make a better choice; and guilt might be telling you that you are not living according to your true values. Never block your feelings – learn to read and follow them.

▼ **NOTICING EMOTIONS**
In this example, a manager reacted to a stressful situation without taking note of her feelings or the feelings of others. It was only when she sought advice that she understood how she could have used her feelings in a positive, constructive way.

CASE STUDY

A manager at a pharmaceutical company was under pressure to meet a deadline. She started working longer hours and demanded that her team work longer hours too.

Within a short space of time, employees were calling in sick. She started to vent her worries at home. Her husband complained that her behaviour was unreasonable and requested that she leave her concerns at work.

She sought advice from her boss, who encouraged her to use her stress to reach a positive outcome. She called a team meeting to explain her predicament. She apologized for her previous unreasonable demands, and she worked with her team to find a solution.

She reflected that if she had recognized the signs of stress in the first place, she could have been proactive about the necessary course of action rather than reacting hastily.

STAYING FLEXIBLE

The ability to be flexible is fundamental to emotional intelligence. Remember that balancing work and life is not just about logic, reason, and finance; it is about heart, soul, and relationships. Aim to see all sides of a situation so that you are less likely to repeat unconstructive habits that only hinder your progress. Learn to be flexible so that you do not succumb to doubt, cynicism, or the temptation to give up.

Face a difficult issue that seems hard to resolve

↓

Stay positive and retain a flexible attitude

↓

Be open-minded and think about all the possible options

↓

Reflect on the possibilities and decide on the necessary action

BEING FLEXIBLE ▶

Flexibility encourages you to stay positive even when a desired outcome looks uncertain. It helps you reflect upon the many options available to you.

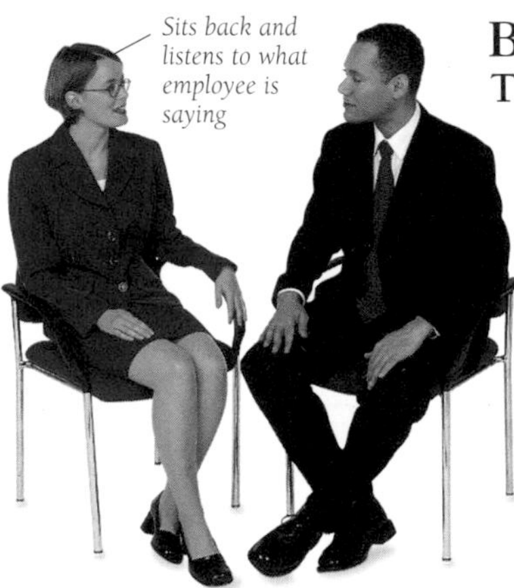

BEING EMPATHETIC

To have empathy means that you are able to understand other people's positions as well as your own. It ensures greater compassion, trust, co-operation, and honesty in your relationships. Begin to identify and let go of any limiting thoughts or feelings you may have that serve to block your success. Always aim to respect and understand other people's positions.

◀ BEING AWARE OF BODY LANGUAGE

By keeping eye contact and an open posture, this manager is showing that she is listening to and acknowledging what the employee is saying. He, in turn, is being open and honest.

DOS AND DON'TS

- ✔ Do show others that you understand and respect them.
- ✔ Do be trusting and open in your relationships with others.
- ✘ Don't make assumptions about other people's feelings.
- ✘ Don't be cynical and inflexible when you are dealing with other people.

30 Recognize doubt in your team members and try to find the cause of concern.

ASKING FOR SUPPORT

It is often counter-productive to keep your feelings to yourself. When you have an emotional issue, seek guidance from a colleague, family member, or friend – someone who is an empathetic listener. Bear in mind that everyone requires support to express their feelings and then learn constructively from them. This enhances self-awareness and self-mastery – the keystones of emotional intelligence. Remember that people with greater clarity about their feelings are more in control of their lives. And if you are effective at managing your own feelings, you will be better able to support others.

31 Listen to others and get a different perspective on life.

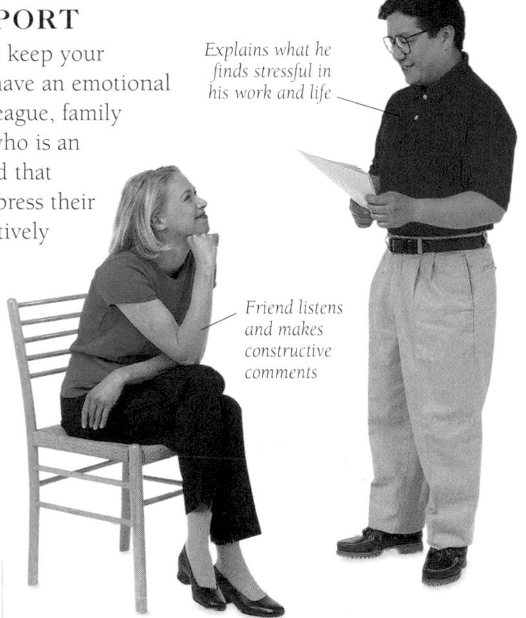

▲ **TALKING ABOUT FEELINGS**

This man has made a list of the things that cause him stress in his life. Discussing them with a friend, and listening to her feedback, helps him deal with issues constructively and positively.

ASKING FOR HELP

Asking for help is a strength, not a weakness. Friends and colleagues may be experiencing similar feelings to you, and talking to them about an issue can help you resolve it. Think about ways you could phrase questions so that you get the positive support you need:

"I have noticed that I start to feel stressed when I have too much work to do. How do you deal with stress?"

"My boss makes comments when I leave work on time. How would you deal with that situation?"

"I am aware that I find it difficult to balance my work and life. What strategies do you use?"

"My son is worried about his school work, but he refuses to talk about it. How would you raise the subject?"

PUTTING TOGETHER YOUR OWN JIGSAW

Your life is like a jigsaw: it is made up of different pieces. Ensure that you make time for each important aspect of your life – your relationships, family, leisure time, work, and self-improvement – and begin to focus on your life as a whole.

32 Remember that good relationships are an essential human need.

ENJOYING A RELATIONSHIP

A poor work–life balance can have a detrimental effect on a relationship. Be aware that if you are unable to shake off the stress of work when you go home, this can affect your private life – and, ultimately, it can cause irrevocable differences between you and those you love. What do you want from a relationship: love, respect, communication, intimacy, fun? How important are each of these elements to you right now? Clarify what you want in your relationship and make achieving that result a priority.

◀ **SPENDING TIME WITH YOUR PARTNER**
This couple schedules time together in which they pursue their mutual interests. Valuing their relationship, they have a balanced home life and, as a result, are better motivated at work.

33 Show your family how much you value them.

DOS AND DON'TS

- ✔ Do seek to understand your partner's needs.
- ✔ Do make sure that you make time to have fun with your family.
- ✗ Don't prioritize your work over your relationships.
- ✗ Don't put off enjoyable activities due to an excessive workload.

HAVING CHILDREN

The experience of parenthood is both demanding and rewarding. Ask yourself what your priorities are in relation to children? Do you have children but want to spend more time with them? Do you want to have children but are unsure about when? Find out your company's family-friendly policies – these could be an important element in your ability to balance parenthood and a career. Recognize that a rich work life and a happy family need not conflict if you are committed to both.

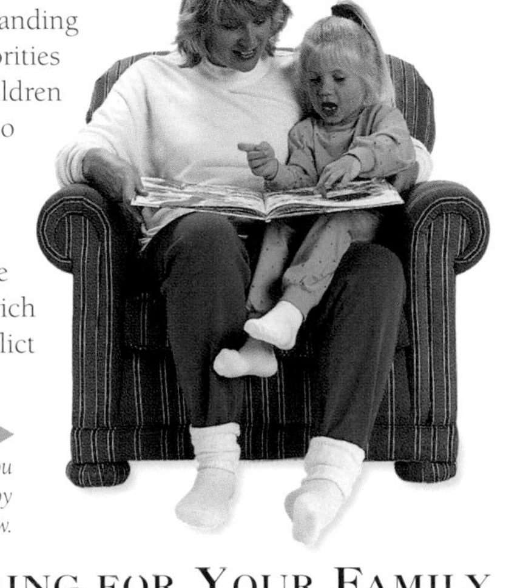

PUTTING CHILDREN FIRST
If you have children, make sure that you spend enough time with them and enjoy helping them learn and grow.

34 Be clear about what kind of parent you want to be.

QUESTIONS TO ASK YOURSELF

Q How important is my family to me?

Q What are my hopes and goals for my family?

Q Do I know what my family wants to achieve?

Q What would it take to improve family life?

Q How can I show my family how much I love and appreciate them?

CARING FOR YOUR FAMILY

View your family – this includes your parents and your friends – as your bedrock. Remember that it is their support that helps you manage the other areas of your life successfully. Be careful not to fall into the trap of neglecting your family and only spending time with them when there is a problem to be resolved. If you repeatedly put work first, a breakdown in communication within the family could occur. Reflect on how important your family is to you: if it figures highly for you, then keep renewing your commitment to it. Schedule quality time together at weekends and evenings. Do not wait for holidays or a birthday before you demonstrate that you care.

35 Recognize the role your family plays in all your successes and how much you rely on their support.

MAKING TIME FOR LEISURE

Do you allow time for your favourite leisure activities? There is a price to pay for not taking leisure time – you may experience higher stress levels, greater exhaustion, ill health, insomnia, and impaired relationships. What leisure activities do you want to do that you may have been putting off? What changes do you need to make to ensure that you achieve a balance? Realize that leisure activities enhance your health by acting as both a preventative measure against stress, for example, as well as a cure for it. A healthy amount of leisure can enrich your creativity at work, your time at home, and your friendships in life.

Plays tennis to take his mind off work and eliminate stress

TAKING THE TIME TO ENJOY SPORTS
Schedule time to play a sport and to take regular exercise – this will keep you healthy, help you unwind, and refresh your mind so that you are ready for new challenges.

36 Use leisure time to help you deal with stress.

37 Realize that taking time to relax will improve your productivity.

DEFINING WORK GOALS

To live a successful, well-balanced life you need to have clearly defined work goals that you can prioritize accordingly. Think about your specific career aspirations. Are you satisfied in your current position or are you planning to make changes? Review your financial aims. Do you want to stay at your current level of salary or do you want to increase your earnings? Do you need to learn new skills to maximize your potential at work? Write down your objectives and priorities.

PRIORITIZING YOUR GOALS
Think about what you want to achieve at work; make a list of your objectives and put them in order of importance; and then set out a plan to work towards.

Clarify your working goals → **List goals in order of priority** → **Plan how you will implement goals**

IMPROVING YOURSELF

It is essential that people commit to lifelong learning in a competitive and fast-moving world. Decide what personal development goals you have. Would it be useful for you to improve skills such as leadership, motivation, communication, or confidence? If so, which ones? Make a personal development plan by listing the key skills that you want to improve and then prioritizing them. Find out what seminars, workshops, or other activities would meet your learning needs. Schedule time to attend events, read literature, and receive coaching.

38 Commit to achieving all your priorities.

39 Set time aside each week for self-development and training.

▼ **PIECING A WORK AND LIFE JIGSAW TOGETHER**

This is an example of a manager's work-life jigsaw. Once she had analyzed the different elements of her life, she began to understand how each aspect fitted in with the full picture of her life.

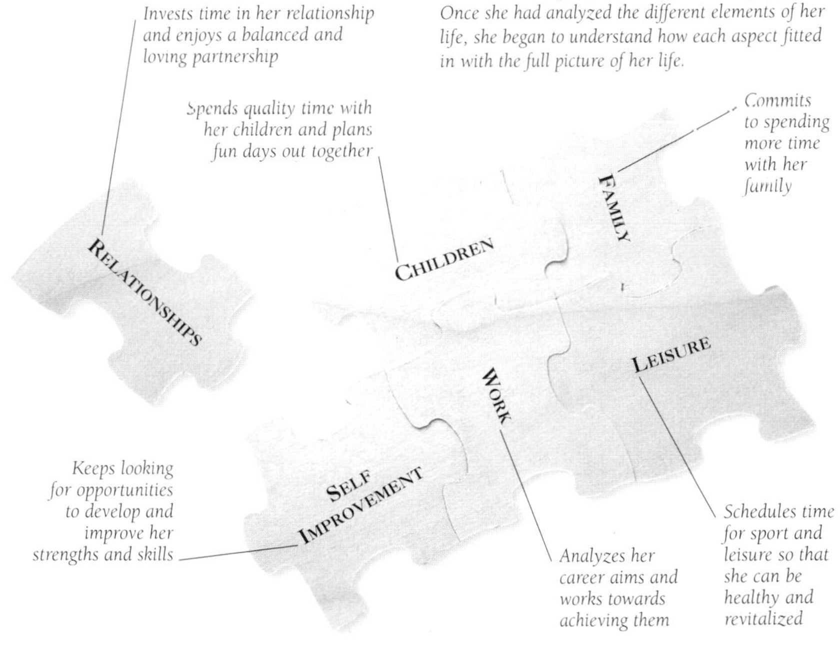

PLANNING ACTION

The key to implementing good intentions is to create and follow an action plan for your work and life. Identify your objectives, clarify your goals, discuss your plans with those who will be involved in them, and set yourself achievable targets.

40 Recognize that action plans save you time, energy, and confusion.

FOCUSING ON OBJECTIVES

Be specific about a final outcome you want to achieve – your objective. Focus on what you do want rather than what you do not want. Think about how you will know that you have achieved an objective. What evidence will you require to show that you have succeeded? Think about what information you will need before you take action and make sure it will not produce any adverse consequences.

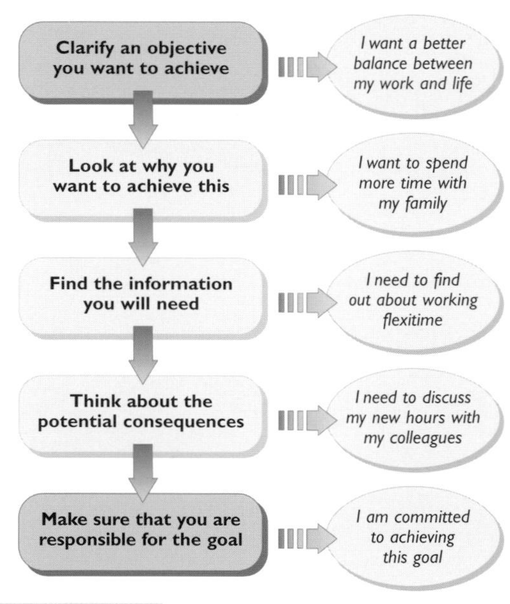

ASSESSING OBJECTIVES
Identify an objective and then think through how you will achieve it before you embark on an action plan.

QUESTIONS TO ASK YOURSELF

- **Q** Am I clear about what I want to achieve?
- **Q** How will I know I have achieved it?
- **Q** Do I need more information?
- **Q** Am I willing and able to take responsibility for my goals?
- **Q** Have I set myself realistic goals?
- **Q** How will I reward myself for successes?

41 Clarify your objectives and then form an action plan.

DECIDING GOALS

Having decided on your desired objectives, clarify the work and life goals that will help you reach each objective. For example, if achieving a work–life balance is an objective, what specific relationship goals will help you reach that objective? What aims do you already have in relation to children? What are your work goals? Review your current goals, or set yourself some new ones.

ASSESSING YOUR GOALS ▶

Make the time to think about your goals. Actively imagine what you will see, hear, and feel when you have achieved them and how they will help you achieve your overall objectives.

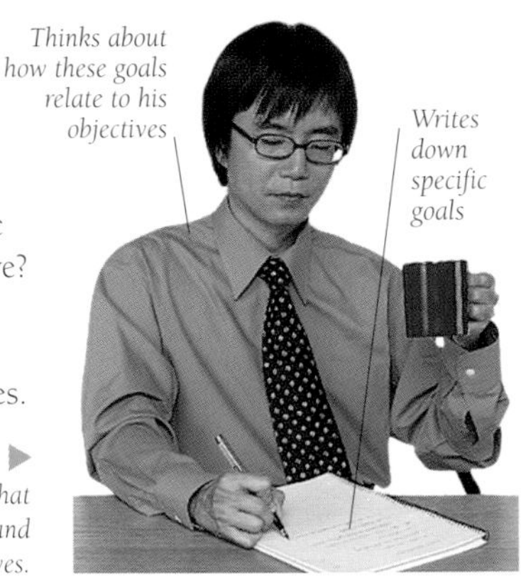

42 Read the latest developments so that all your actions are well-informed.

GATHERING INFORMATION

Before you start work on your goals, ensure that you are as well informed as possible. The right information can save you a lot of time and energy. Make use of all the resources around you, such as colleagues, a human resources manager, your friends, inspirational books, training courses, the internet, or a coach. There is no need to reinvent the wheel. Get as much information and help as you can and make every action an informed choice.

KNOWING WHO

You will achieve your goals if you ask for support from the appropriate people. Identify the key players in your situation. Discuss your plans and ask for their input when necessary. Some people can feel threatened by change – try and understand their concerns. Reassure them that you have thought through your actions, but be flexible and ready to consider other options.

INVOLVING KEY PEOPLE

COLLEAGUES
Talk to your colleagues and ask for their input and advice when necessary.

PARTNER
Discuss and agree your plans with your partner.

FRIENDS
Talk over your ideas with your friends and be open to new options.

DECIDING STEPS

It is vital to identify clearly how you will achieve each goal before you take action so that you stay focused. Break down each goal into bite-sized chunks and prioritize each chunk. The more understanding that you have about the sequence of events that will lead to an outcome, the easier it will be to achieve. Ask for a second opinion on the steps you have recognized, and if necessary, involve the appropriate people in particular steps.

POINTS TO REMEMBER

- People do not plan to fail, they fail to plan.
- If plans become outdated, be flexible and look for alternative solutions.
- It can be motivating to tell someone your action plan.
- Whenever you make a plan, always take at least one action immediately.

43 Set a date for each of your action steps.

MANAGING YOUR TIME

Identify realistic time frames for actions so that you can pace yourself, stay focused, and measure your progress. Remember, if your ultimate aim is to achieve a better balance between work and life, it defeats the object to set unrealistic targets that create unnecessary pressure on you. Establish your key objective and then do something every day, however small, to move towards it.

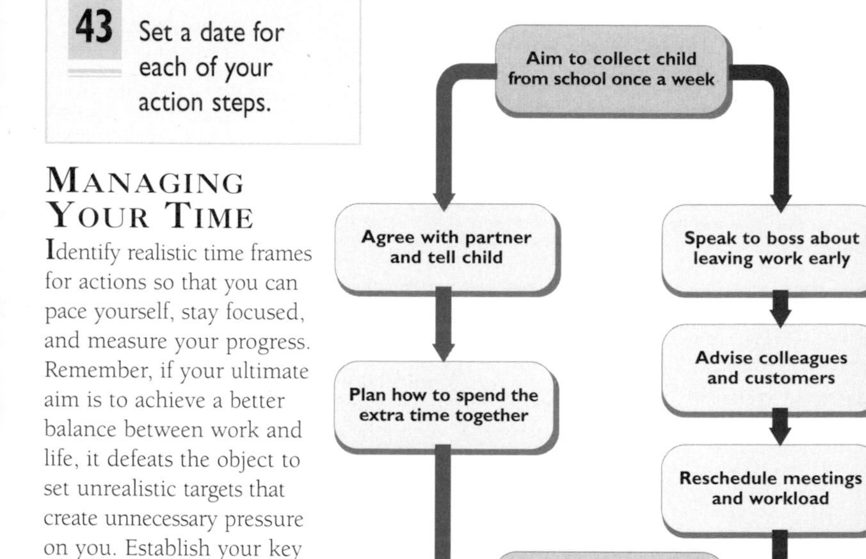

SCHEDULING ACTION STEPS ▲

In this example, a manager has decided that he wants to spend more time with his child. His goal is to collect his child from school once a week and share a leisure pursuit. He defines the steps he needs to take at home and at work, and puts them into sequence.

Key

 *Action steps to be implemented at home*

Action steps to be implemented at work

MAKING A PLAN TO ACHIEVE WORK–LIFE BALANCE

GOAL	INFORMATION NEEDED	STEPS TO TAKE	DEADLINE
RELATIONSHIPS To work together as a team with my partner	To talk to my partner about both our needs, and look at how we could communicate more effectively.	• Arrange a romantic dinner. • Set time aside for a frank discussion.	April 20th
CHILDREN To read them a story three times per week.	Find out what stories my children like, and make sure that I can leave work punctually to be home at their bedtime.	• Ask children what stories they like. • Start leaving work on time.	April 15th
FAMILY To enjoy a family activity at least once a week.	To have a family discussion about what activities each of us enjoy and what types of hobbies we could do together.	• Discuss mutual interests. • Agree on shared activities.	May 1st
WORK To spend most of my time on important tasks.	To talk to my manager to help me clarify my role and to find out what my most crucial day-to day tasks are.	• Review my work tasks and priorities. • Speak to my boss about my priorities.	April 10th
LEISURE To have a tennis lesson once a fortnight.	To find out about local tennis coaches, convenient times for lessons, and what prices they charge.	• Call a coach. • Schedule regular tennis lessons and attend.	May 7th
PERSONAL DEVELOPMENT To learn meditation.	To ask my friends and colleagues to recommend a good meditation course, either near my home or my office.	• Find a convenient class. • Schedule a meditation course.	May 14th

MAKING CHANGES

There are practical measures you can take to create a better work and life balance. Think about changes, start to put them into action, and lead your team through your good example.

ADAPTING WORK ROUTINES

To be successful in today's workplace, organizations and employees have to be open to new ways of working. Notice how globalization, new technology, and new employment trends are forcing change, and look at ways of adapting your work routine.

44 Realize that everyone benefits when you balance your work and life.

45 Set a target for the number of hours you want to work.

46 Make sure you always take all your allocated annual leave.

ACHIEVING BALANCE

Organizations who actively promote work-life strategies benefit from better recruitment and improved staff retention – their staff suffer from less stress and take less sick leave. The economy also benefits because the job market stabilizes, giving more people the opportunity to work. Society benefits because parents can more easily provide for the health and happiness of their families. Realize that a good work–life balance is beneficial for all, because individuals who achieve this balance tend to perform better, enjoy good health, and achieve sustainable success.

KNOWING THE LAW

By law, employees are entitled to a set amount of annual leave, and maternity or paternity leave; they are also entitled to compassionate leave. An organization cannot normally require employees to work more than a set national number of hours a week – employees may choose to work longer, however.

WORKING HOURS

Decide how many working hours a week are right for you. Some people want to work fewer hours, for example, to accommodate higher education. Others may prefer to work more hours so that they can earn extra income. Clarify your objectives so that you can make better decisions about your career. Consider part-time options such as job-sharing, where two employees share one job; term-time working, where an employee has leave during school holidays; and "V" time working, where an employee works reduced hours with the guarantee of returning to full-time work later.

WORKING FROM HOME

Home working is where employees agree to do some or all of their work from home. They usually make a dedicated space for work at home and also share "hot desks" or "flexi desks" at the office. New technology has made home working more possible in recent years – it is especially suited to jobs like computer programming, market research, and journalism. Before you opt for home working, make sure that you are able to set clear boundaries between work and the rest of your life.

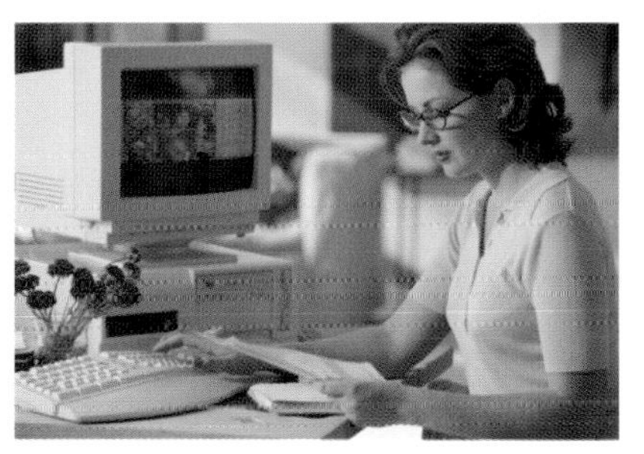

▲ **WORKING FROM HOME**
The benefits of working at home include no commuting time, more actual working time, flexible working hours, and more time with your family.

47 Find out about your entitlement to maternity or paternity leave.

WORKING FLEXIBLY

Flexible working schemes are becoming more common. "Flexitime" allows you to set your own daily working hours. "Flexi-leave" means you can break annual leave into long-weekends and half-days. "Compressed hours working" allows you to work the hours of a normal five-day week within four days. "Annualized hours" allows you to work a set number of hours each year in your own time. Find out what options are available to you.

WORKING SMARTER, NOT HARDER

A common myth is that the results you achieve are directly related to how hard you work. However, greater effort does not always equal greater effectiveness. Use your time efficiently, learn to delegate, and make sure you switch off when you leave the office.

48 Value every hour of the day – make sure that you use them effectively.

49 Take full advantage of your available leisure time.

50 Schedule regular hour-long thinking sessions.

USING TIME EFFICIENTLY

Sometimes a poor work–life balance is a symptom of poor time management. Realize that time is your most valuable resource: ultimately, your ability to "save time" or "waste time" determines how well you balance your work and life. Have you ever systematically recorded and assessed your work time? Do you employ an effective time-management system to plan your working week? Take a moment now to identify one "time vampire" that eats into your available time and, also, one "time saver" that can win you back some time.

TIME-SETTING TIPS

There are habits you can develop to help you use your time more effectively at work and improve your productivity:

- Monitor and review your time at work to make sure you are working efficiently.
- Break tasks into manageable sizes, and schedule them accordingly.
- Prepare daily activity sheets to identify your key priorities, meetings, and deadlines – make sure that your team members have access to these.
- Create a diary on your computer, update it daily, and refer to it to make sure that you are on track.
- Encourage your team to make their own decisions, rather than referring to you about every issue – there is not enough time in the day.

TIDYING YOUR WORK AREA

Decluttering your work area encourages mental clarity and sharper focus so that you are better able to deal with your workload. Schedule time each week to declutter your office and master your desk. Your desk surface should be reserved only for current, high-priority projects. Get a large wastepaper bin and purge your desk-top and drawers of any unnecessary paper. Make sure that your computer filing system is up to date and easy to navigate around.

51 Set aside one hour every week to tidy your workspace.

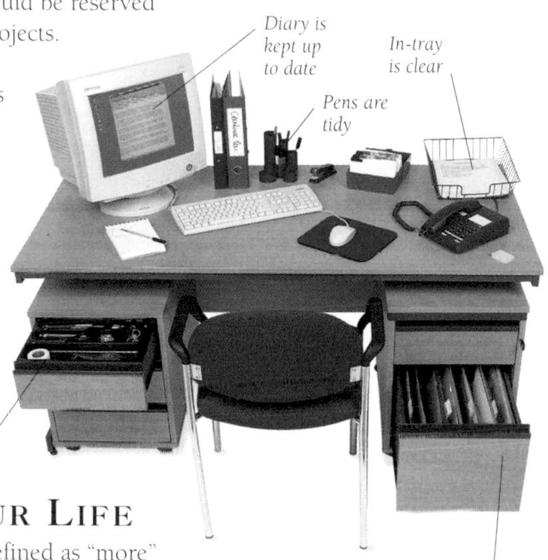

KEEPING ORGANIZED ▶
Make sure your in-tray is free of paperwork – file away correspondence that you have already dealt with. If you have redundant files on your computer desktop, delete them.

SIMPLIFYING YOUR LIFE

Success has traditionally been defined as "more" – more money and possessions, a car with more horsepower, a job with more responsibilities, a social life with more friends. Recognize that too much of "more" can clutter up your life. It can leave you over-stretched, over-committed, and overwhelmed. Avoid losing sight of your true values and real priorities. In this way, you can let go of excess and focus on what is most essential.

52 Evaluate your real priorities and focus your attention on them so that you are able to give your best.

THINGS TO DO

1. Think about what is essential to you.
2. Find out whether your colleagues' priorities conflict with your own.
3. Plan solutions that take into account everybody's particular needs.

DELEGATING EFFECTIVELY

One of the biggest blocks to enjoying a healthy work–life balance is the failure to delegate. Recognize that if you are able to delegate effectively, you will have more time and space to set your own goals and to organize, manage, and coach your team. Delegation ensures that no-one is indispensable, it gives colleagues opportunities to grow and to prove themselves, and it helps managers evaluate potential. Remember that positive delegation means that you have enough time and energy to steer your team towards its true purpose and success. It also ensures that you do not drown in over-tiredness and, in the long run, let your team down.

ASSESSING YOUR WORKLOAD

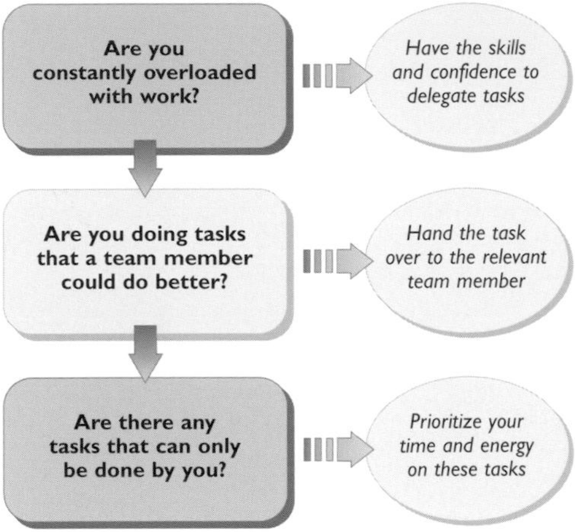

Are you constantly overloaded with work? → *Have the skills and confidence to delegate tasks*

Are you doing tasks that a team member could do better? → *Hand the task over to the relevant team member*

Are there any tasks that can only be done by you? → *Prioritize your time and energy on these tasks*

53 Decide whether it is necessary for you to do a task personally or if it is possible to delegate it.

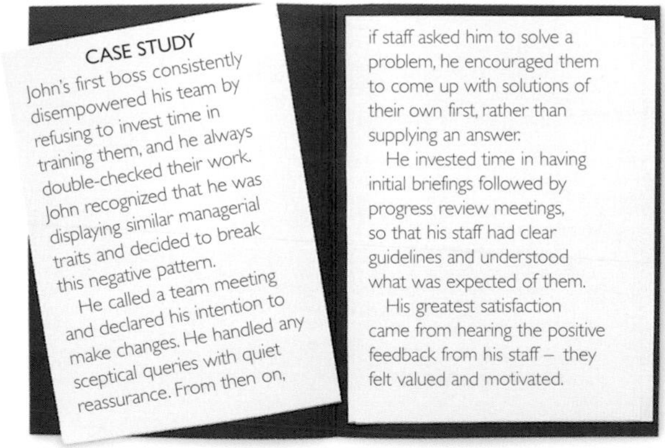

CASE STUDY

John's first boss consistently disempowered his team by refusing to invest time in training them, and he always double-checked their work. John recognized that he was displaying similar managerial traits and decided to break this negative pattern.

He called a team meeting and declared his intention to make changes. He handled any sceptical queries with quiet reassurance. From then on, if staff asked him to solve a problem, he encouraged them to come up with solutions of their own first, rather than supplying an answer.

He invested time in having initial briefings followed by progress review meetings, so that his staff had clear guidelines and understood what was expected of them.

His greatest satisfaction came from hearing the positive feedback from his staff – they felt valued and motivated.

◀ LEARNING TO DELEGATE

A manager was creating a cycle in which his inability to delegate was producing a negative outcome. He consciously decided to change this habit. He found it difficult at first, but each success made it easier and he soon found that the habit of delegating became automatic.

SWITCHING OFF

Leave your work behind when you leave the office. Clearly designate what is "work time" and what is "family time", "time out", and "my time". If you do this, you will probably find you work fewer hours but produce more focused work. When "work time" is over, learn to stop thinking about it. Discipline yourself to turn off mobile phones, pagers, laptop computers, e-mail, and the internet. This will help refresh your mind and body. Aim to live more and work better.

▲ **LEAVING WORK CARES BEHIND YOU**
When you leave work, and are enjoying time out with your friends, leave any work issues behind you so that they cannot invade and disrupt your personal life.

Switch off → **Relax** → **Recharge**

▲ **TAKING TIME FOR YOURSELF**
When you leave the office each evening, switch your mind off from your work. Take quality time to rejuvenate, and you will feel refreshed and better equipped to deal with work the next day.

QUESTIONS TO ASK YOURSELF

- **Q** Am I using my time effectively or is there a better way I could organize myself?
- **Q** Is there an easier way I could approach this task?
- **Q** Could I delegate this work to someone who would be better able to deal with it?
- **Q** Do I spend enough time on priorities, or am I distracted by other tasks?
- **Q** Do I create enough time and space for family and friends?
- **Q** Do I allocate any time for reviewing, revising, and improving working practices?

ONE-MINUTE EXCELLENCE

Punctuate your daily work schedule with moments of quiet. Take one minute of excellence to review goals, strategy, and balance: one minute is often enough to give you an idea that can help you work smarter, not harder. Ask yourself questions, like, "Is this the best use of my time?" and "Is there a better way to do this?" Give yourself "time out" to make sure you are not being distracted by urgent, but unimportant, tasks.

UNDERSTANDING CHANGE

Understanding the psychology of change can help you make changes for the better. Be specific: think about the changes you could make, the people who could offer you support, the obstacles you may encounter – and then take action.

54 Have the courage to make changes in your work and your life.

CULTURAL DIFFERENCES

It is part of the Japanese culture to be adaptable to continual change. Europeans, on the other hand, are generally less open to change, although this attitude is slowly altering. In the United States, they approach change as a challenge. Australasians often initially resist change, but then tend to adapt to it very well.

BEING OPEN TO CHANGE

Change is inevitable in life, whether you actively seek it or try to avoid it. You can deal with change in two primary ways: either resist it or welcome it. Bear in mind that resistance to change usually creates more problems than it avoids. It can cause greater fear, anxiety, procrastination, and imbalance. You can feel stuck, and your life will not move forward. Recognize that resistance is not a solution, and that your life will not change if you will not change. Instead, have courage and welcome change. Take a leap of faith and make adjustments for the better by being willing to take a risk. If you adopt a proactive approach to change, it will pay dividends.

BENEFITING FROM CHANGE

To make a change happen, you must get leverage: this means that you must understand how change will affect you. You can do this in two ways. Assess the cost of not making a change for the better in your work and life balance. What will be the cost to your quality of life, your relationships, and your effectiveness at work? Alternatively, assess the benefits of making the change. How much happier will you be? How will your family and friends feel? How much more rewarding will work be? Use your answers as leverage to help motivate you to make changes.

55 Be proactive and work to make things happen.

56 Take responsibility for the changes you want to happen.

CREATING CHANGE

Identify what it is you want to change. Be specific. What is it about your work and life balance that you want to improve? Is it fewer working hours, more free weekends, less commuting? Next, ask yourself who do you need to speak to about it? Is it your manager, colleagues, customers and/or your partner? What new action will you undertake? Will you delegate more, attend fewer meetings, or stop saying "yes" to unessential tasks?

57 Ask yourself what changes you could make to your life.

▼ IDENTIFYING ISSUES

Instead of thinking about a problem in a negative way, think about how you could approach it positively, and come up with a constructive solution.

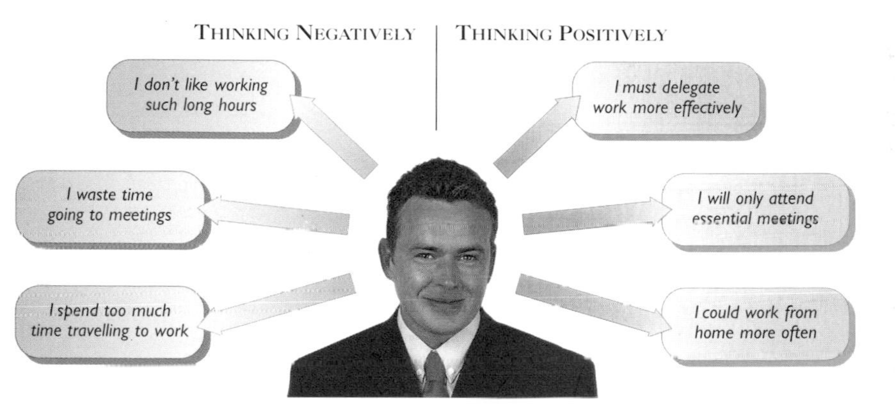

SAYING "NO" TO UNESSENTIAL TASKS

Many people continually find themselves overloaded with work because they find it difficult to say "no". Realize that you can change this pattern: If you know that you will not have the time to deal with something, be honest:

"I would like to help you, but my current list of priorities is taking up all my time."

"Are you absolutely sure you need my input at this stage? If not, please come back to me at a later date."

"I understand that the schedule is tight, but my own project is delayed. Can someone else help you?"

"I'm sorry that I am unable to deal with your task, but I can offer advice that may be of use instead."

POINTS TO REMEMBER

- Unhealthy independence can cause you unnecessary struggle and create setbacks that could have been avoided.
- People who are too independent are usually afraid to ask for help when they need it.
- It is a sign of strength, not of weakness, to ask for help.

FINDING SUPPORT

A common block to making changes is unhealthy independence. If you try to make changes entirely under your own steam, you can block yourself off from other people's encouragement, support, and inspiration. Take a moment to make a list of all the people who might be able to support you in having a better work–life balance. Make a list of other possible sources of support, such as books, training courses, and specialist networks.

RECOGNIZING OBSTACLES

Internal obstacles to change, such as fear of failure, usually outnumber external obstacles, such as an uncompromising boss. To create a change, let go of your old patterns of thinking and behaving. Let go of old doubts and fears. Once your mind is clear, you will be in a better position to address any external obstacles you may face – and these are often not as insurmountable as you imagine.

58 Ask a coach or mentor to help you deal with a change you want to make.

OVERCOMING INTERNAL OBSTACLES TO CHANGE

INTERNAL OBSTACLE	SOLUTION
SELF-DOUBT I feel awkward about initiating this change.	Acknowledge your doubts but recognize that you do not have to face change on your own.
FEELING OVERWHELMED I can only handle so much change.	Keep yourself focused on the benefits of the change you are making.
INNER FEARS I lack the confidence to make this change.	Ask for feedback from a trusted colleague to assess the reality of your concerns.
NEGATIVE THINKING In the past, changes have backfired.	Remember an occasion when you were forced to make a change, but it worked out well.

TAKING ACTION

The key to making any change is to begin: one small step is enough to start the ball rolling. Either you can act or you can wait for something to happen. Waiting for a change to happen is called procrastination, and this is a major block to change. Procrastination is a thief of time. It stops you from taking responsibility for your life. It corrupts creative thinking, decision-making, and proactive living. Decide what change you want to make, get leverage, ask for help, address the obstacles, and then decide to act. Ask yourself, "What is the next best step I could take to achieve a better work–life balance?" and "When will I take this step?" Schedule a date in your diary and stick to it.

59 See that small changes make a big difference.

60 Challenge every obstacle that you encounter.

▼ MAKING CHANGES

Once you have pinpointed a change you want to make, and have worked to eliminate any possible obstacles, you are ready to implement it.

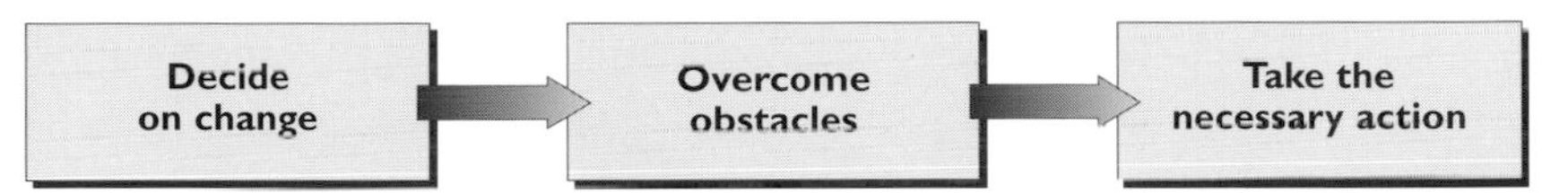

DEALING WITH ▶ OBSTACLES

A manager had witnessed many changes within her organization during a short period of time. She was cynical about a further change her boss had outlined, but she had to rise to the challenge.

CASE STUDY

Kim, a manager in the communications industry, was asked by her boss to increase sales, but without an equivalent increase in resources.

She was cynical about being able to increase the sales figures, but she called her team together and informed them of the position. She listened to their concerns and ensured that they felt understood. She encouraged their creative input and followed up their ideas.

Although Kim took the leadership role, she involved everyone in decision-making, because she realized that this was essential for the team's ongoing commitment. She noted how ready each team member was to the proposed change and encouraged the risk-takers to lead. Kim then kept focused on managing the change and its outcome.

Together, Kim and her team successfully achieved the seemingly impossible results.

LEADING BY EXAMPLE

Managers are most effective when they act as a role model and lead by example – in this way, they bring out the best in themselves and others. Create a good team culture, coach your team, and ensure that your staff maintain a work–life balance.

61 Be a good example to your colleagues and team members.

LEADING THE WAY

An effective manager is a good role model. Make sure you lead by action and not just words – always demonstrate what is required. Remember that people learn best by example. As a manager, you are in a position to teach and demonstrate the importance of a healthy work and life balance. Think about how you might best do this. For example, leave the office on time so that you encourage your staff to do likewise.

▲ A GOOD ROLE MODEL
Be an example to your team by implementing a good attitude, a strong set of values, and proactive behaviour. As you display these qualities yourself, you will inspire your team to go the extra mile.

DOS AND DON'TS

- ✔ Do take your full lunch break and leave work on time.
- ✔ Do look after your health and spiritual wellbeing.
- ✔ Do take your allocated holiday leave and use it constructively.
- ✔ Do schedule time for leisure activities.

- ✗ Don't book meetings after office hours.
- ✗ Don't always be the last person to leave the office.
- ✗ Don't send e-mails to colleagues at the weekends.
- ✗ Don't ignore your commitments to your family.

62 Make sure team members respect each other.

63 Tell your team what you expect from them.

GIVING GUIDANCE

As a manager, it is your job to steer the team culture – this is a set of agreements about how best a team will work together. When you are creating a team culture, focus on vision, values, relationships, and key issues such as work–life balance. Be explicit about what you want. Tell people you want them to be effective rather than exhausted. Make sure that your team members know that you do not require them to give their all for the job at the expense of their home lives. Reinforce a work–life balance every time you conduct interviews, give feedback, do performance reviews, or lead team meetings.

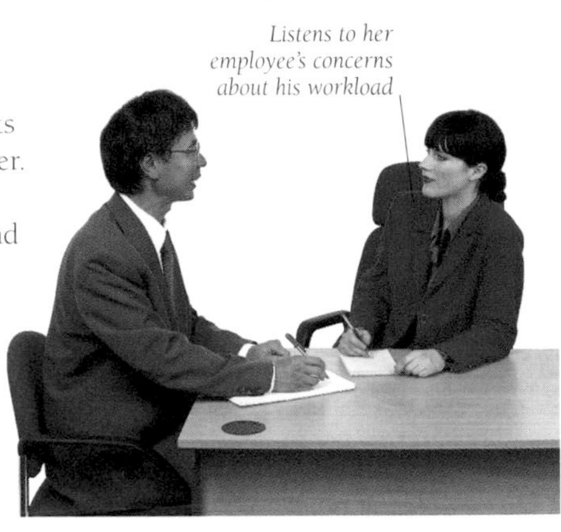

▲ GIVING A REVIEW
During a performance review, take the opportunity to talk to your team members about their work–life balance and suggest ways that it could be improved.

64 Monitor the motivational level of your team.

BUILDING HEALTHY TEAMS

It is not in a manager's interests to have a continually overworked team, because the cost of overworking is too high. Teamwork deteriorates, performance falters, relationships suffer, and the team spirit eventually dries up. Monitor the health of your team, keep gauging their energy, and be alert to the dangers of burnout. If you drive your team to exhaustion, they will not be able to produce the results you need and you will lose their loyalty. Make sure that team members are able to be creative and are given the chance to offer ideas.

Manager listens to ideas

Sales assistant suggests possible new database

◀ ENCOURAGING IDEAS
Establish a culture that supports and encourages the creativity of your team, so that team members feel valued and fulfilled by their work.

CULTURAL DIFFERENCES

In the United States and Japan, annual leave is generally shorter than in Europe. Britain has a reputation for working long hours. Meanwhile, in France, employees are not expected to work more than a 35-hour week.

BANISHING GUILT

A "guilt culture" is one of the biggest drains on personal effectiveness at work. The term refers to the pressure people feel to work long hours, work weekends, skip lunch breaks, forgo holiday leave, and miss family commitments. Guilt cultures are often perpetuated by managers and team members, but organizations pay a high price in return. Realize that overworking blunts performance and long hours do not necessarily increase productivity. Banish guilt and liberate the talent of your team.

COACHING OTHERS

For a team to work well, each team member must work to their own optimum personal effectiveness. Coach your staff to have a better work–life balance. Coaching may include one-to-one sessions, time-management training, or making helpful information available. Remember, the right balance between work and life varies between people. Build rapport, listen, understand, and then create a programme to suit individual needs.

65 Teach others what you want to practise yourself.

66 Encourage your team members to leave the office on time.

BALANCING TEAM WORKLOADS ▼

Each week, meet with your team and schedule the week's work. Let team members discuss their workload and, if necessary, share out responsibilities so that no-one is overstretched.

Sales executive explains that he forsees problems meeting deadline

Sales assistant is willing to help with workload

Manager suggests sales executive delegates work to sales assistant

COACHING TECHNIQUES

Coaching is a valuable skill that you can use in one-to-one sessions with your staff, and in your daily interactions with people. Aim to gain rapport and trust because this is the first step in good communication. Remember that the key to effective listening is being able to see situations from other people's points of view. If you are working with a coachee, help them create a well-formed action plan to follow. Make sure that you clearly outline the steps, timing, and people involved in any action.

BEING A COACH ▶
Listen to the coachee, but also give constructive feedback. Offer advice if you are asked, but let the coachee develop his or her own solutions.

RESETTING THE BALANCE

Remember that it is in your interests that your team members have healthy home lives. Of course, business does sometimes involve unpredictable change, crises, busy seasons, unforeseen meetings, difficult deadlines, weekend conferences, and travel abroad. A work–life balance is not static and is always changing – there will be times when home life suffers. Be quick to reset a healthy work–life balance as soon as possible. Don't just push on. Remember, balance is the key to sustainable long-term success.

67 Rest when your energy is low so that you recharge.

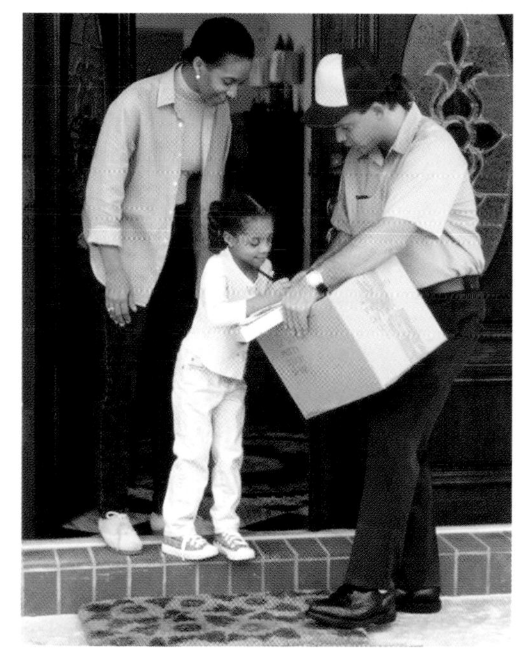

▲ ACKNOWLEDGING GOOD WORK
When your staff have worked long hours to meet a difficult deadline on a project, be quick to thank them and their families for their extra efforts – you could even send a hamper.

SUSTAINING BALANCE

Maintaining balance is the key to professional and personal success. Be sure about what you want, live a healthy and fulfilled life, stay motivated, and always celebrate successes.

REVIEWING YOUR GOALS

Regularly reviewing your goals can help you focus your time and energy on what is most important to you. Set yourself achievable goals, make sure you evaluate all your experiences, and keep checking that you are focused on your priorities.

68 Review your purpose regularly so that you remain focused.

LIVING WITH PURPOSE

Your purpose is the reason why you take action. It is like a compass that helps you navigate the way ahead. If you do not review your purpose regularly, you can lose your direction, impetus, and *joie de vivre*. Be clear about why you go to work and what you want from your life. Write down your purpose and keep referring to it. Ensure your goals and actions align with your purpose.

◀ **DISCUSSING YOUR VISION**
Discuss your purpose with friends and colleagues in order to build greater mutual understanding and support, and to learn from their experiences and insights.

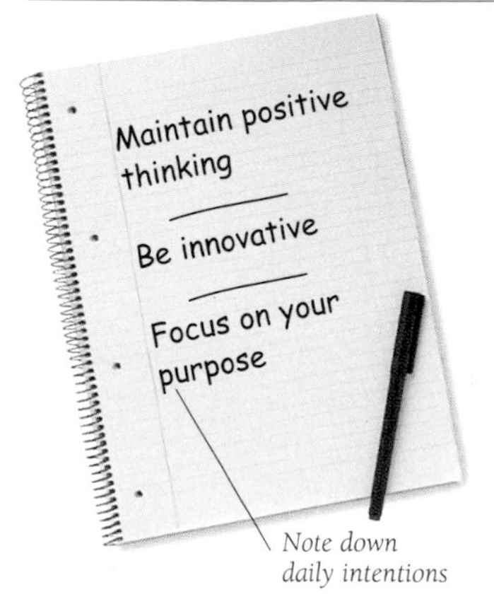

Note down daily intentions

FORMING INTENTIONS

An intention is a specific mental focus to help you achieve an outcome. Each day, set intentions for the type of person you want to be, the life you want to live, and the contribution you want to make. Let these intentions inspire your actions, choices, and thinking. On difficult days, you may need to keep reminding yourself of your intentions because it is easy to be swayed off your course.

◀ **FOCUSING ON YOUR INTENTIONS**
Write down your intentions. Read them before you make a phone call, type an e-mail, or go to a meeting so that you are constantly reminded of what you are aiming to achieve.

PAYING ATTENTION

There is an old saying: "some people go through life, and others grow through life". Successful people are committed to lifelong learning and growing. By being willing to learn and grow, you will not be a victim of life. Pay close attention to the results you get in life and use every experience as a learning curve. Make time to evaluate your experiences. Ask yourself, "What is the lesson here?" and, "What do I need to learn here?" Look at every problem as an opportunity and every challenge as a chance to learn something new.

69 Remember that positive thinking is more effective.

70 Write your reflections in a daily journal.

QUESTIONS TO ASK YOURSELF

Q Have my values and priorities remained the same, or are they changing?

Q Am I having enough time for myself?

Q Who could I be spending more time with?

Q Am I taking my family's views into account?

STAYING FOCUSED

Once a week, schedule time to review your work and life. Ask yourself key questions and listen to your intuition. Think about your goals and ask yourself, "Are my actions in line with my priorities?" Think about your day and ask yourself, "Am I making the best use of my time?" Think about your relationships and ask yourself, "How could they improve?" Think about your health and ask yourself, "Do I have enough leisure time?" Use the answers to your questions to sharpen your focus.

BEING ASSERTIVE

Assertiveness helps you to align your thoughts, communications, and actions. Make sure that you know what you will say "yes" to and what you will say "no" to, always be true to yourself and others, and put your assertiveness into action.

71 Be certain about what you want and what you do not want.

72 Dedicate your valuable time to your real priorities.

73 Be assertive about saying "yes" to your priorities.

SAYING "YES"

True assertiveness starts with knowing what you want to say "yes" to. Every day you are exposed to numerous opportunities, invitations, choices, advertisements, requests – all of which want a "yes" from you. Avoid trying to say "yes" to everything because you will end up unfocused and unable to fulfil your commitments. Make sure that you know what you want to say "yes" to, so that you can be effective, happy, and purposeful. Saying "yes" to your priorities commits you to what is important in your life.

▼ **PRIORITIZING LEISURE TIME**

This manager views leisure time as a priority. When a colleague approaches him and proposes a game of squash during a lunch hour, he responds enthusiastically.

Colleague suggests a game of squash

Manager agrees to play squash

SAYING "NO"

If you cannot say "no" you may lose sight of your purpose and focus. A difficulty in saying "no" can lead to confused priorities, unhealthy compromises, inner exhaustion, and general ineffectiveness. Learn to say "no" – this will save time for you and others. It will make your relationships stronger and more honest.

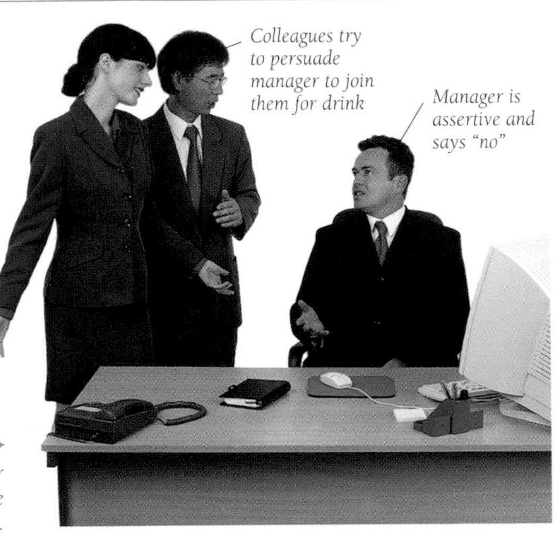

BEING DEFINITE ▶
When his colleagues ask this manager for a drink, he would like to join them, but he would prefer to spend some time at home.

74 Think about how you react to someone who is direct, honest, and authentic.

BEING AUTHENTIC

Many people find it difficult to say "no" because they think it will cause conflict, anger, and guilt. If, however, you never say "no" you will lose focus and respect and, ultimately, you will lose yourself. Recognize that this inauthenticity can lead to deceit and resentment. You will find that the more authentic you are, the more honest and helpful others will be in return. Be assertive so that you are authentic and true to yourself.

ACTING NOW

Assertiveness is an antidote to procrastination. Focus your attention on the present, instead of on the future. Set "present-time goals" – something that can be achieved immediately. First, decide what is important to you, such as being a good friend. Next, ask yourself questions such as, "What can I do today to be a good friend?" Think about the action you could take to achieve your goal, and put it into effect immediately.

THINGS TO DO

1. Set a "present-time goal".
2. Take immediate action so that your good intention is not lost.
3. Monitor progress to ensure that the goal is achieved.

DEVELOPING CONFIDENCE

Inner confidence enables you to make decisions and take actions that help you sustain a healthy work–life balance. Learn to value and believe in yourself, build on your strengths, and aim to be resourceful, decisive, and empowered.

75 Recognize that if you respect yourself, others will too.

POINTS TO REMEMBER

- If you treat yourself well, others will treat you well too.
- The way you view yourself is expressed in your posture and your body language.
- When you behave decisively and confidently, people will follow your lead.
- A happy, balanced life starts with self-belief and vision.

76 Make a list of your strengths and aim to add to it.

VALUING YOURSELF

It is up to you to value yourself and your life. If you will not do this, then no one else can either. Remember that you have a lot to give, but you can only do this if you appreciate yourself. One way to value yourself is to ensure you sustain a healthy work–life balance. Remind yourself that you are a valuable asset to your organization, your colleagues, your family, and your friends. Look after yourself. Remember that the better you treat yourself, the more you can achieve. People will respect you for valuing yourself, even if it feels unfamiliar to them initially.

▼ **ASSESSING YOUR CONFIDENCE**

When your confidence is low, your lack of self-esteem will show in your tense facial muscles. As your confidence rises, your bearing and expressions become more positive.

BUILDING SELF-BELIEF

Self-belief immunizes you against hopelessness and feeling dis-empowered. Remember that the greater your confidence, the greater your capacity will be to take action and succeed at life and work. Develop your self-belief, and your abilities, skills, and strengths will increase too. Adopt a "can-do" mentality and you will achieve your goals. Remember, a healthy work–life balance is always possible: believe you can do it, and you can.

77 Recognize that being assertive and positive helps you sharpen your focus.

BUILDING STRENGTHS

The more you build on your strengths, the easier it is to build your work–life balance. Perform the SWOT analysis on yourself. Look at your strengths. What are you already skilled at? Next, identify your weaknesses. What could you improve? What fears could you let go of? Next, spot opportunities for change, growth, support, and help. Finally, look for any threats that might hamper your progress, such as procrastination and self-doubt.

◀ **USING THE SWOT ANALYSIS**
Use the SWOT analysis to help you focus. Take an honest look at your strengths and weaknesses. Look at ways you could change or grow and examine the possible obstacles in your way.

EMPOWERING YOURSELF

Empowerment increases assertiveness, inspires creativity, and supports effective action. It can also help you to be decisive and resourceful when too many demands compete for your time and energy. Symptoms of dis-empowerment include lack of inspiration, low energy levels, and a sense of hopelessness. Usually you will feel dis-empowered when you are acting without purpose. When you feel this way, ask yourself, "What needs to happen for me to be empowered again?" Get support for making the necessary changes.

78 Think about what makes you feel empowered.

79 Work on your inner beliefs and they will grow.

DEALING WITH STRESS

Stress is an increasingly common feature of modern living. Avoid perceiving stress as the "enemy" – think of it as a possible "friend" that can help you to sustain a work–life balance. Learn to deal with stress and anxiety, and aim to have fun!

80 Learn to recognize the signals your body makes when you are stressed.

THINGS TO DO

1. Recognize the symptoms of stress.
2. Make a point of choosing to think positive thoughts.
3. Schedule regular exercise, to help cleanse your body.
4. If your muscles are tense, take a warm bath.
5. Find someone to talk to about your worries.

BUSTING STRESS

Stress is like a red light that appears on the dashboard of your car. It is a signal telling you that you are "running on empty" and are "out of balance". Whenever you are feeling stressed, recognize that your body is telling you to make a change for the better. If you do not take action, you will receive louder and more frequent signals. Recognize stress as a sign that your work–life balance is under threat – use it as an impetus to act.

▼ **TRACKING CAUSES OF STRESS**

Monitor the things that make you feel stressed during the week, such as giving a presentation or leading a meeting, so that you can learn to cope with these events in a more positive way.

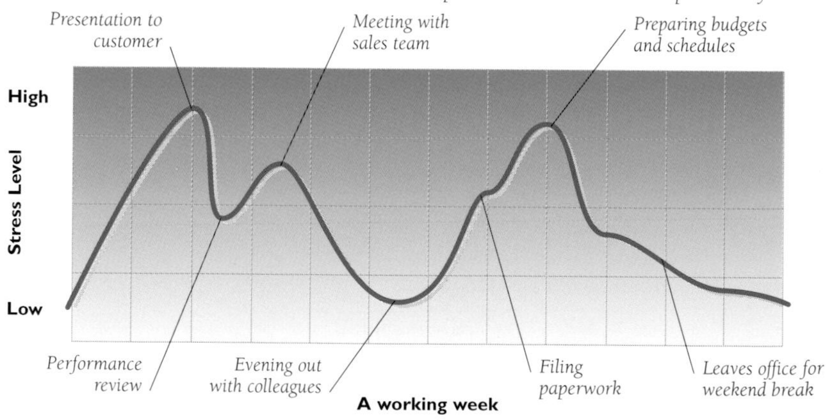

ALLEVIATING ANXIETY

How much anxiety does it take to solve a problem? None, because anxiety is not a solution for anything. Instead, anxiety is a sign for you to take action. Identify the cause of your anxiety. Note down what will happen to you if all you do is stay anxious. Write down the possible things you could undertake to counteract your anxiety. Decide on the appropriate action and begin it now.

QUESTIONS TO ASK YOURSELF

Q Why am I feeling anxious and what can I do to alleviate the feeling?

Q What is the root cause of this anxiety?

Q Would it help to talk to someone about this?

81 Give yourself time to relax and recentre every day.

82 Try not to take every issue too seriously.

ENDING STRUGGLE

Struggle is not always inevitable or necessary. Sometimes people struggle and they make things harder than they need to be. They invite struggle because they refuse to ask for help, make a change, or try to feel relaxed. Be aware that struggle is a state of mind. People who are continually battling often believe that struggle is an inevitable price for success and happiness. Whenever you are struggling, ask yourself how you could do things more easily. Use your imagination and intelligence to find an easier way.

HAVING FUN

The "fight, flight, or frolic" responses are three ways to deal with stress. Choose the "fight" option and tackle stress head on. For example, communicate more honestly with someone you have been avoiding. Opt for the "flight" option and remove yourself from the stress. This may involve taking a lunch break, going for a walk, or having a holiday. Choose the "frolic" option and concentrate on work, rest, and play, play, play.

▲ **TAKING TIME TO ENJOY YOURSELF**
If you are feeling stressed, take the time to have fun. An evening out can help you wind down and will immunize you against stress – this in turn will help you be more effective at work.

LIVING HEALTHILY

Good health is all about balance. Improve your work and your life by ensuring that you eat nourishing food, exercise regularly, and sleep well. Notice when your mind and body are feeling low on energy and take the time to rejuvenate.

83 Make sure that you keep your body properly nourished.

CULTURAL DIFFERENCES

The Japanese government advises its citizens to eat at least 30 different types of food each day so that they obtain the necessary amount of nutrients in their diet. Western governments are now aware that diets high in salt and saturated fat are a major cause of disease in their countries.

EATING WELL

Hippocrates, the father of medicine, wrote, "Let your food be your medicine, and let your medicine be your food". Make sure that you make healthy choices about your diet. Educate yourself about food, your body type, and the most healthy diet for your lifestyle. Eat plenty of fruit and vegetables during the day so that you have a rich source of vitamins and minerals. Make sure that you get the right balance of carbohydrates, protein, and fats. Limit your intake of artificial additives and sweeteners and your daily intake of caffeine and alcohol. Try to drink two litres of water per day.

TAKING EXERCISE

Either you have to take time to be healthy or you have to take time to be ill. Recognize that regular exercise is a great way to increase health, boost your energy, have more fun, switch off from work, and have an active social life. If you have not exercised for a while, a gym instructor can test your fitness level. He or she can also plan a personal programme that will help you improve your fitness level. Get into the habit of scheduling exercise sessions into your diary just as you would plan an evening out with friends. What exercise have you planned for this week? Get your diary out and book something now.

84 Ensure you eat three regular meals per day.

85 Book regular coaching sessions in your favourite sport or hobby.

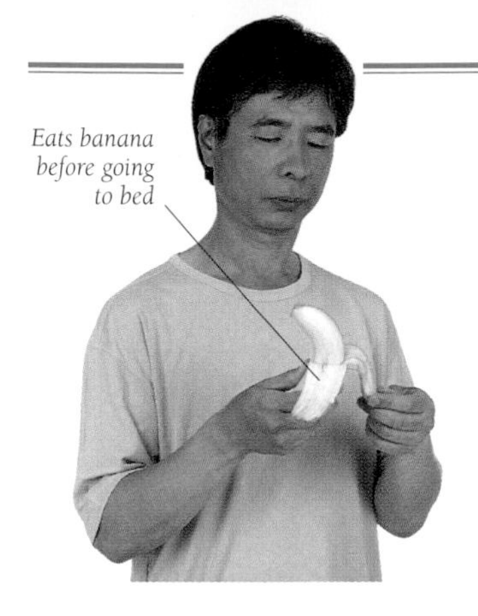

SLEEPING BETTER

Adults require an average of eight hours of sleep a night. In the long term, sleep deprivation can lead to mood swings and poor concentration. Are you sleeping well? Do you feel rested when you wake? A common cause of sleep disruption is a drop in blood sugar levels during the night. Try having a non-sugary snack before you go to bed.

◀ HELPING YOURSELF SLEEP
If you have problems sleeping, eat a banana an hour before bedtime – the fruit contains tryptophan, which has natural sedative powers that will help you relax and sleep more soundly.

RELAXING REGULARLY

Being able to relax is vital for a good work–life balance. Discover which ways of relaxing you prefer. Some people like to practise meditation, read quietly, or have long hot baths. Other people prefer more active and social types of relaxation, such as playing sports, going to the cinema, or enjoying a meal with friends. Relax regularly and you will boost your health, enjoy your life more, and improve your performance at work.

86 Relax before you go to bed – light some scented candles and have a bath.

RELAXED BREATHING EXERCISES

Try these breathing exercises before you go to sleep, or during moments of stress:

- Sit or lie down in a comfortable position. Ensure your head, neck, and spine are aligned. Close your eyes.
- Allow your breathing to become deeper, longer, and slower.
- Breathe into the abdomen area, pushing your stomach out as you breathe in and letting your stomach sink back down again as you breathe out.
- End your relaxation as deliberately as you began. Repeat when required.

RELAXING ▶
As you inhale, repeat the words to yourself "deep and long and slow". As you exhale, repeat the words "slow and long and deep".

Increasing Your Vitality

Vitality is a by-product of balance, health, and happiness. Boost your vitality by looking after yourself and by making good choices. Live your life to the full, enjoy your work and your leisure time, and have a positive and happy outlook.

87 Celebrate and enjoy the fact that you are alive each day.

THINGS TO DO

1. Commit to spending time with the people you love.
2. Schedule time with your friends in your diary and stick to the dates.
3. Choose social events you want to attend.

Living Life to the Full

Do you live to work or do you work to live? Life is an adventure. Have the courage to take risks, break routines, and be spontaneous so that you can enjoy new experiences. Live for today and embrace happiness now – if you give yourself wholeheartedly to life, you will actually increase your vitality. Once you do, you will find that you work better because you will approach challenges with more energy. Remember that life is too precious to waste.

Enjoying Your Work

When work is no longer fun, it can lead to stress and unhappiness. Aim to make your work fun so that you increase your creativity, enhance your relationships, and become more successful. It may be necessary to change your job. Or try viewing your job from a positive perspective – most jobs have something to do with helping others, being of service, or making a difference. Recognize the value of your job and learn to enjoy your work.

88 Discover what you are passionate about and make sure that you try and incorporate it into your work.

Questions to Ask Yourself

Q What aspects of my work am I passionate about?

Q What is my purpose at work, and what do I hope to achieve in my career?

Q How could I make work more enjoyable, rather than viewing it as a chore?

Q How could I be more creative at work?

Q How could I make more of a difference at work?

Q Is there a better attitude I could approach my work with?

ENCOURAGING LEISURE

Use your leisure time to put the zest back into your life. Schedule activities you enjoy and take the time to learn new interests. After a stressful day at the office, it can be invigorating to do something completely different. Find yourself what psychologists describe as "a third place" – a place other than home and work where you can unwind and enjoy yourself, such as a tennis club, a sailing club, an art class, or a coffee bar.

89 Plan days off work regularly so that you can recharge.

▼ **ENJOYING A HOBBY**
Learn a new skill, and you will feel challenged and rewarded. Your brain will be reinvigorated, giving you the energy and focus to inspire your work and life.

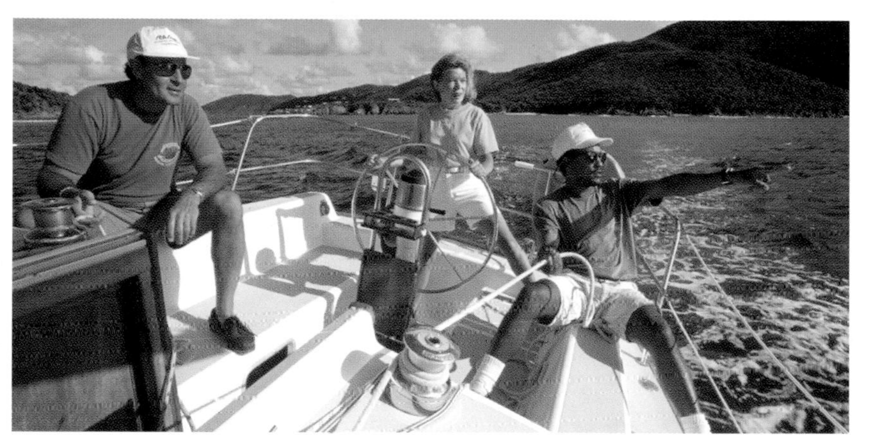

90 Develop a positive outlook and your life will be happier.

91 Notice how people react to your positivity.

CHOOSING HAPPINESS

Vitality is as much a mental attitude as a physical state. One of the biggest drains on your energy can be inner fears, self-criticism, and cynicism. By contrast, there is nothing more energizing than laughter, a compliment, or a moment of kindness. Sometimes it can be tiring if you are trying too hard to feel happy. Avoid chasing happiness. Instead, make sure you choose happiness by changing your outlook and state of mind. Make a conscious decision to be happy and to enjoy your life, and choose a better balance in your life.

STAYING MOTIVATED

It is easy to be motivated when your work and life are both going well, but it is also important to keep motivated when you are faced with challenges. Overcome any problems, ask for help if necessary, and give yourself the chance to be inspired.

92 Make sure your attitude is part of the solution, not the problem.

OVERCOMING DIFFICULTY

Everyone experiences bad times. Most people know what it is like to fail an interview, lose a customer, or argue with a friend. Success is not about the absence of failures: it is about the courage to overcome them. Try not to feel demotivated during difficult times – this can create a downward spiral of apathy and negativity. Hold your nerve and stay positive so that your attitude does not make a difficult situation worse.

Remains positive and focused, and strives to succeed

ACTION

FOCUS

ATTITUDE

BELIEF

COURAGE

STAYING POSITIVE ▶
Even during difficult situations, keep your mood and momentum upbeat. Adopt the positive qualities that will bring you success.

93 Get feedback from your colleagues and customers.

94 Look for solutions and, if necessary, ask for help.

ASKING FOR HELP

If a situation feels too much to handle on your own, it probably is. In other words, you probably need some extra help. Trying to stay motivated every day all by yourself is almost impossible. Life and work is a team game. Remain strong by being willing to ask for and accept help. During difficult times, spend quality time with people who understand you, support you, and believe in you – such as your family and friends. Realize that too much self-reliance can be a weakness.

TAKING CHARGE

During difficult times, ask yourself, "Is this something I can change?" In other words, find out if you are willing to take charge. Are you taking responsibility or are you making excuses? Are you waiting for things to get better or are you taking action? Are you blaming others or are you looking for solutions? When you are faced with a problem, reset your thoughts, choices, and perceptions and focus them on success, not on failure. Change your thoughts and you will transform your life.

QUESTIONS TO ASK YOURSELF

Q Do I know someone who could be my mentor?

Q Do I regularly read inspirational books to feed my imagination?

Q What training course could I attend next?

Q Who could give me valuable feedback?

95 Choose your thoughts carefully – remain focused.

96 Make sure that you note down inspirational ideas.

BEING INSPIRED

What do you do for inspiration? Do you listen to motivational tapes? Do you find inspiration in nature or in meditation? Most people do not get their best ideas at work. In fact, they are often most inspired when they are relaxed and detached from work. Make space in your life for inspiration. Carry a small notebook and write down any ideas as they occur to you. Book meetings and lunches with people who you admire and can learn from. When you travel, go by train instead of by car so that you can read, reflect, and relax more.

◀ **NOTING IDEAS**
Even when you are out with colleagues or friends, make a note if someone says something that inspires you, or a good idea occurs to you.

CELEBRATING SUCCESS

When you achieve a success, make sure you celebrate it – celebration builds your confidence, increases your future resolve, and helps make success a state of mind. Recognize, reward, enjoy, and share success in yourself and others.

97 Keep a "success journal" and note down your daily achievements.

98 Recognize successes at home as well as at work.

99 Reward team members for their successes.

RECOGNIZING SUCCESS

Do you notice when you have done something well, or do you generally only notice when you have got something wrong? Are you quicker to praise than you are to find fault? The ability to recognize your success and the success of others is an essential skill for building a success-focused culture within your team. Realize that recognition is motivating. Ensure that you identify your own success and encourage your team to do the same. Start meetings by acknowledging recent successes, rather than merely discussing failures or mistakes.

REWARDING SUCCESS

Do not fall into the trap of waiting for an annual performance review or another form of systemized approach to reward success. Sometimes people feel that if they reward success too frequently, it will lose its meaning. They forget that even a simple "thank you" is an important, under-used reward that costs nothing. Ensure that you have ongoing incentive schemes that reward your employee's achievements. Monitor the schemes to make sure that they raise morale and yield the desired effect of showing that you value good performance. Reward your own successes too – buy yourself a gift, treat yourself to a meal, or go to a health spa to show that you value yourself.

THINGS TO DO

1. Notice when a team member completes a task well.
2. Let them know that their success has been noticed.
3. Set up an incentive scheme to reward staff achievements.
4. Reward yourself for your own triumphs and successes.

100 Celebrate with your family so that they feel involved in your success.

ENJOYING SUCCESS

Many people achieve successes but fail to enjoy them. There are many reasons for this. One is the tendency to push ahead so fast to the next goal or task that there is no time for celebration. Another is that they undervalue themselves and their achievements. Maybe they feel that completing a project successfully is merely part of their job description. Make sure that you enjoy your success and reward yourself with a healthy work–life balance. It is not worth having success at work if you have no friends, no fun, and no life.

SHARING SUCCESS

There is no such thing as a self-made man or woman. Success is always a team effort. When you are successful in life and in work, share your success with those who count. You can do this in many ways, such as by sharing your learning, giving others your support, and thanking people for their contribution. Helping others will remind you of your own skills. Teach others what you want to learn. Remember that a good work–life balance is achieved through mutually supportive relationships at work and at home.

101 Have the courage to choose the life you want to lead.

▲ CELEBRATING WITH COLLEAGUES

Success is an ongoing process, not a final goal. Celebrate success with your team at significant points during a project, not just at its completion, so that you sustain morale and motivation.

ASSESSING YOUR WORK–LIFE BALANCE

Find out how well you manage your work–life balance by responding to the following statements. Mark the options that are closest to your experience. Be as honest as you can: if your answer is "never", mark Option 1; if it is "always", mark Option 4, and so on. Add your scores together, and refer to the Analysis to see how you scored. Use your answers to identify areas that need improvement.

OPTIONS

1 Never

2 Occasionally

3 Frequently

4 Always

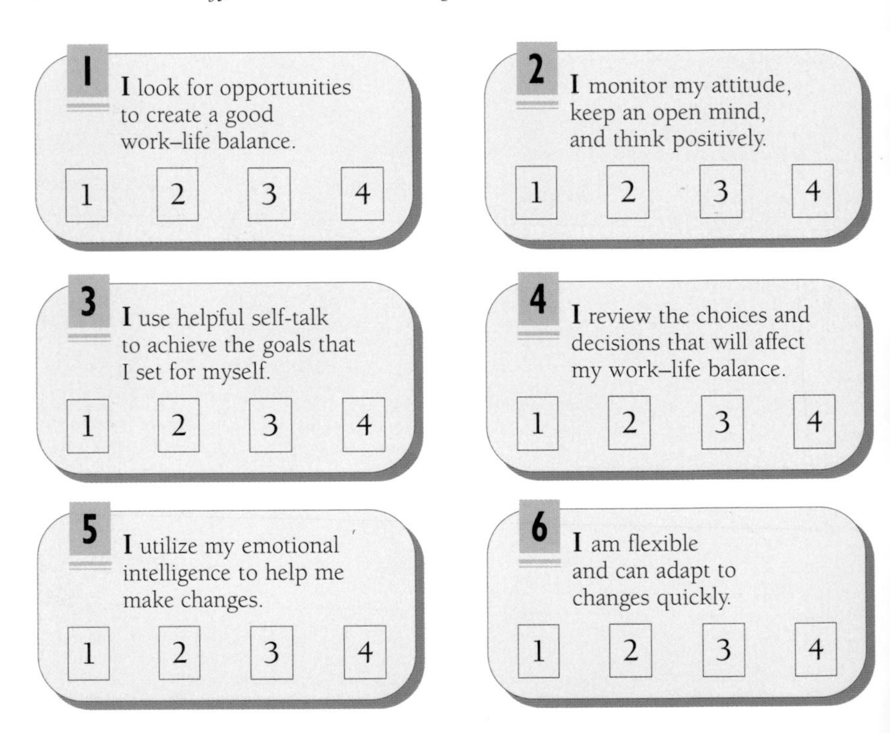

7

I prioritize my loving relationships and put them at the centre of my life.

1 2 3 4

8

I spend rewarding, quality time with my family and friends.

1 2 3 4

9

I schedule a healthy amount of leisure time each week.

1 2 3 4

10

I clearly identify my key objectives before I take action.

1 2 3 4

11

I use a structured action plan to achieve my objectives.

1 2 3 4

12

I invest time and energy in communicating effectively with others.

1 2 3 4

13

I seek to understand other people's points of view.

1 2 3 4

14

I try and find solutions that are best for everyone involved.

1 2 3 4

15

I have meetings with my team to generate new and creative solutions.

1 2 3 4

16

I am proactive about making changes for the better.

1 2 3 4

17

I identify the best working options that match my objectives.

1 2 3 4

18

I avoid "starting early, finishing late" on the majority of work days.

1 2 3 4

19

I do not make a habit of taking work home to finish at night.

1 2 3 4

20

I rarely go into the office to work at weekends.

1 2 3 4

21

I use my time away from work effectively and make the most of my leisure.

1 2 3 4

22

I take responsibility for my choices and actions.

1 2 3 4

23

I recognize that I am constantly learning and developing my skills.

1 2 3 4

24

I make time for the most important people in my life.

1 2 3 4

25

I know what I want to say "yes" to in my work and in my life.

1 2 3 4

26

I believe in my ability to achieve my goals and objectives.

1 2 3 4

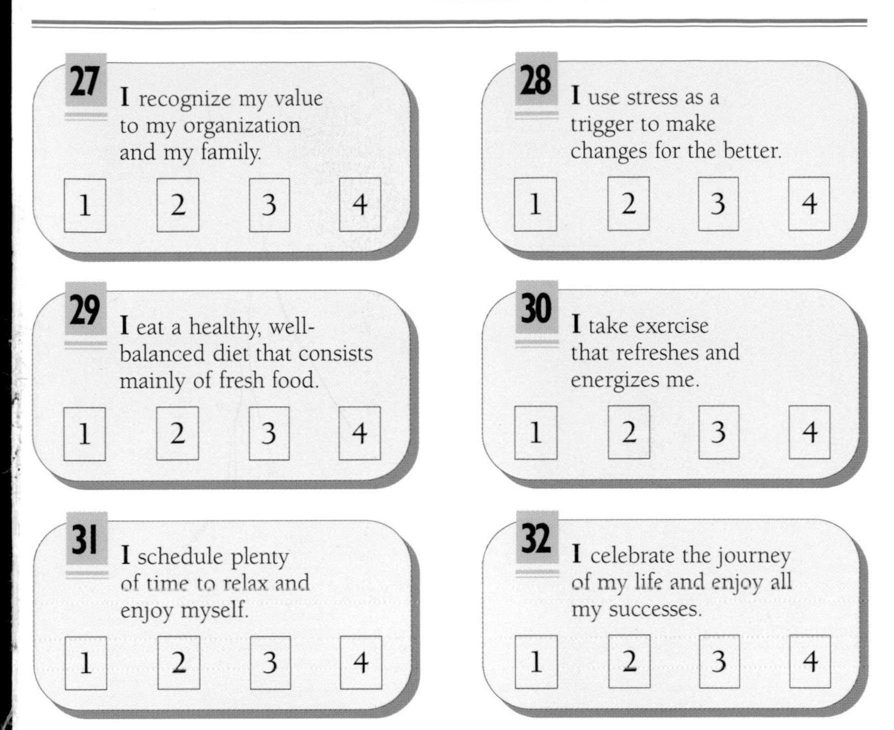

27 I recognize my value to my organization and my family.

1 2 3 4

28 I use stress as a trigger to make changes for the better.

1 2 3 4

29 I eat a healthy, well-balanced diet that consists mainly of fresh food.

1 2 3 4

30 I take exercise that refreshes and energizes me.

1 2 3 4

31 I schedule plenty of time to relax and enjoy myself.

1 2 3 4

32 I celebrate the journey of my life and enjoy all my successes.

1 2 3 4

ANALYSIS

Now you have completed the self-assessment, add up your total score and check your work–life balance by referring to the corresponding evaluation below. Identify your weakest areas, and refer to the relevant sections in this book to develop and hone those skills.

32–62: You are working too hard and need to examine your priorities. Implement the strategies in this book to try something new and improve your work–life balance.

65–95: To make changes for the better you need to know how, and you must want to. You are doing well, but allow yourself the chance to enjoy even more balance.

96–128: You are focused, well-motivated, and have a clear direction. Remember: work–life balance is an ongoing process, so keep refining your skills.

INDEX

ACKNOWLEDGMENTS

AUTHORS' ACKNOWLEDGMENTS

Real success is a team effort. Thank you to Adèle Hayward at Dorling Kindersley for her vision and dedication. Thank you to Kate Hayward at Studio Cactus for her editorial expertise and encouragement, and Laura Watson at Studio Cactus for her design skills and creativity.

PUBLISHER'S ACKNOWLEDGMENTS

Dorling Kindersley would like to thank the following for their help and participation:

Editorial Amy Corzine; **Indexer** Hilary Bird; **Proofreader** Polly Boyd; **Photography** Gary Ombler

Models Roger André, Philip Argent, Angela Cameron, Kuo Kang Chen, Russell Cosh, Carole Evans, Richard Hill, Vosjava Fahkro, Kate Hayward, Cornell John, Brian Monaghan, Chantal Newell, Lois Sharland, Kerry O'Sullivan, Suki Tan, Gilbert Wu **Make-up** Nicky Clarke

Picture researcher Anna Bedewell, Mariana Sonnenberg; **Picture librarian** Melanie Simmonds

PICTURE CREDITS

The publisher would like to thank the following for their kind permission to reproduce their photographs:

Key: a=above; *b*=bottom; *c*=centre; *l*=left; *r*=right; *t*=top
Corbis: 4/5c; Walter Hodges 57br; James Marshall 61c
Getty Images: David Hanover 6bl; Paul Viant 37cr;
The Stock Market: 49br
Stone: Chad Slatterly 41tr
Telegraph Colour Library: 50bl

AUTHORS' BIOGRAPHIES

Robert Holden is the founder of The Coaching Success Partnership. His services are retained by entrepreneurs, sportspeople, and others worldwide. His programmes, such as *Success Intelligence*, *Liberating Talent*, and *Coaching Success* are used by leading businesses everywhere. His innovative work is featured by two major BBC television documentaries (*QED: Happiness* and *QED: Stress Busters*). He has written nine best-selling books, including *Shift Happens!* For more information, visit www.happiness.co.uk

Ben Renshaw is co-director of The Coaching Success Partnership. He travels the world coaching leaders in the field of business, sport, education, and healthcare. He is a leading relationship expert, and his seminars such as *Relationship Intelligence* and *The Motivation Effect* are in high demand. He makes regular media appearances, including on the Channel 4 television documentary *Perfect Match*. His best-selling titles include *Successful, But Something Missing*. For more information, visit www.happiness.co.uk